I can be a

Science Detective

Claudia Martin

ARCTURUS

ARCTURUS

This edition published in 2019 by Arcturus Publishing Limited
26/27 Bickels Yard, 151–153 Bermondsey Street,
London SE1 3HA

Author: Claudia Martin
Illustrator: Katie Kear
Editor: Donna Gregory
Designer: Jeni Child
Art Direction: Rosie Bellwood

ISBN: 978-1-78888-496-9
CH006571NT
Supplier 29, Date 0719, Print run 8648

Printed in China

What is STEM?

STEM is a world-wide initiative that aims to cultivate an interest in Science, Technology, Engineering, and Mathematics, in an effort to promote these disciplines to as wide a variety of students as possible.

Contents

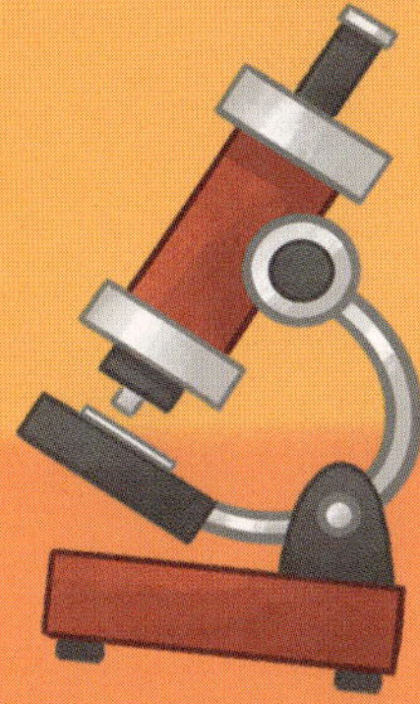

Always Be Prepared!

Do you want to use your science skills to solve crimes? This is what forensic scientists do. They collect evidence from the scene of a crime, and then they do tests to try to discover when it was committed and how—and who might have done it.

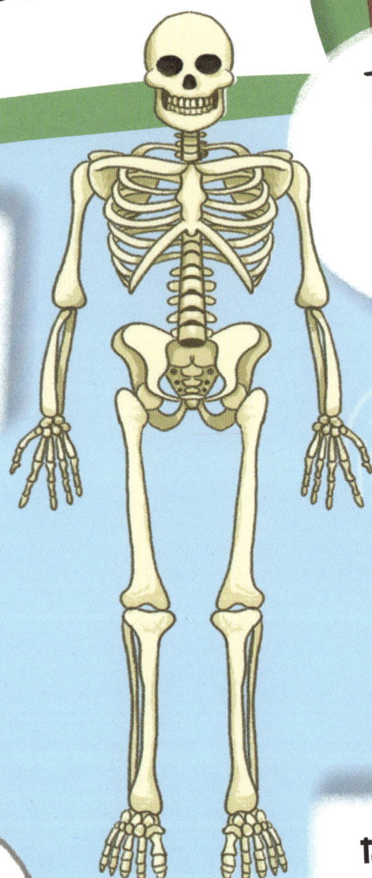

The criminal may have left traces at the crime scene—this is called "trace evidence!"

Knowledge of the human body might give us clues about the criminal.

Tests can reveal if the criminal used itching powder, explosives, or even poison!

Broken glass, splatters, and car tracks reveal how the crime was commited.

Project: Pack Your Bag!

Before you head to your first crime scene, pack your bag. As well as equipment for collecting evidence, you need to take a clean body suit, face mask, and gloves, so you don't leave traces of yourself at the scene.

Equipment for Collecting Evidence:

- Camera
- Chemicals for tests
- Crime scene suit
- Evidence bags and labels
- Fingerprint brush and powder
- Gloves
- Magnifying glass
- Mask
- Notebook and pen
- Test tubes
- Tweezers

Which of these bags contains everything on the list?

Find Fingerprints

The skin on your fingertips is covered in patterns of tiny ridges. When you touch shiny surfaces, your sweat leaves a mark in the shape of these fingertip patterns, called fingerprints.. Forensic scientists can see these prints more clearly by dusting them with powder.

Each person has a slightly different set of patterns. If there are fingerprints at a crime scene, you might be able to identify who made them!

Although your fingerprints are unique, the same types of shapes show up in everyone's prints. They're called arches, loops, and whorls.

Project: Take Your Prints

When police officers arrest a suspect, they often make a record of their fingerprints using ink and paper. Try recording your own fingerprints! Can you see any arches, loops, or whorls?

You will need:

- Two pieces of white paper
- A blunt pencil
- Tape
- Scissors

1. Use a pencil to scribble on paper, going over the same area again and again.

2. Rub a clean, dry fingertip over the patch.

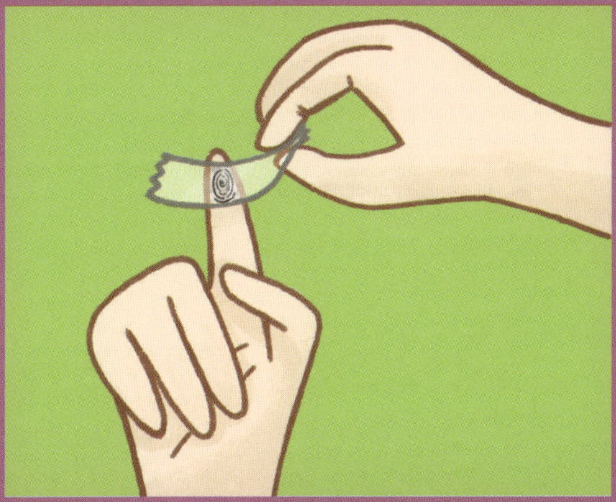

3. Stick a piece of tape over the fingertip, then pull gently away. Now you have a record of your print.

4. Stick the tape onto a clean piece of paper and label it. Repeat steps 1–4 with your other fingers —or with friends and family.

Examine Footprints

Sometimes footprints are left by a criminal at a crime scene, often pressed into mud. Scientists can record these prints by filling them with liquid plaster, which will harden into a solid. Then they can compare them to the shoes of suspects to place them at the scene.

Different types or brands of shoes have slightly different patterns on their soles.

Take a look at the soles of your shoes. The prints left by your shoes are almost as unique as your fingerprints.

Everyone walks differently, by scuffing their heels or pressing harder with the outsides of their feet.

Project: Who Ate The Cookies?

Someone has eaten all the freshly baked cookies on Fairmeadow Farm. Follow the footprints and use your crime-solving skills to find out which suspect ate them!

Suspect 1
Farmer Fiona

Suspect 2
Farmer Fred

Suspect 3
Sam the Sheepdog

Suspect 4
Percy the Pig

Suspect 5
Gertrude Goose

Suspect 6
Merlin Magpie

Collect DNA

Cells are the tiny building blocks that make up your body. Nearly every cell in your body contains long, thin molecules of DNA. DNA contains the instructions that tell your cells exactly how to grow and function. These are passed down from parents to their children. They tell your body to have one head and a beating heart, and to have, for example, red or black hair, and brown or blue eyes.

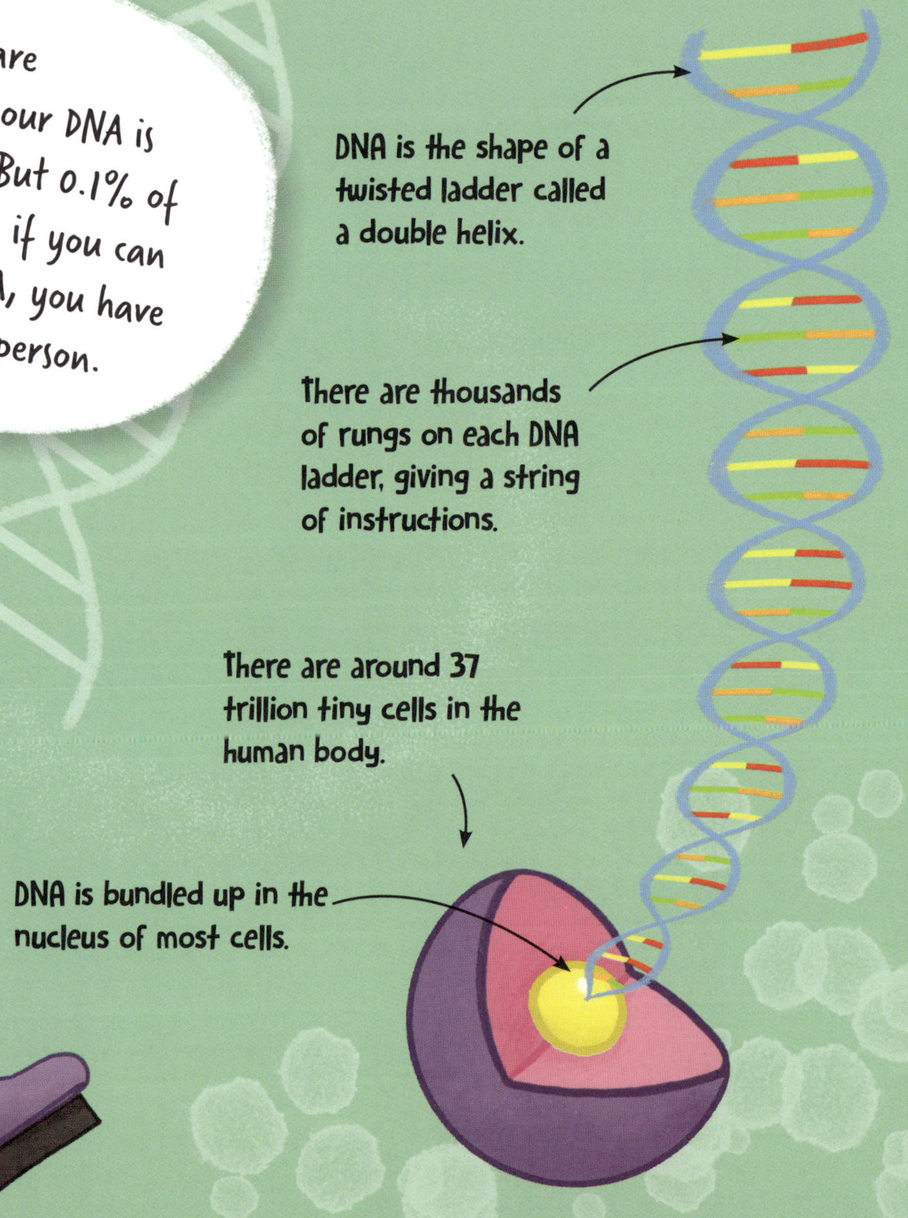

Project: Search for Samples!

Forensic scientists can find DNA in flakes of skin, nail clippings, and hair. They can also collect it from body fluids, such as blood, sweat, vomit, tears, earwax, pee, poop, saliva (dribble), and mucus (snot). Grab your evidence bags, and circle 5 items in this hotel room that might contain DNA samples.

... And Examine DNA

When forensic scientists have collected material containing DNA, they take it to a lab. First, they extract, or take out, the DNA from its cell. Then they study the DNA to see if it matches up with DNA taken from suspects.

Studying someone's DNA cannot tell us exactly how they look or behave, because human beings are very complex. But here are 5 things that DNA can tell us about an unknown suspect:

1. If they are likely to have light (e.g. blue, green), dark (brown and black), or hazel eyes.

2. If they are likely to have red hair.

3. If they are the same person as, or in the same family as, someone who has already given a DNA sample.

4. If they are male or female.

5. If they have a high risk of suffering from certain diseases that are passed through a family's DNA.

Project: Extract DNA From a Strawberry

Strawberry cells contain lots of DNA molecules—much more than human cells—so they are quite easy to extract and see. A single molecule of DNA is too thin to see with the naked eye, but this experiment makes the strands of strawberry DNA clump together so we can take a look.

You will need:

You will need an adult to pour and measure the rubbing alcohol!

- 15 ml (1 tablespoon) rubbing alcohol or surgical spirits, chilled
- 90 ml (6 tablespoons) water
- 10 ml (2 teaspoons) dishwashing liquid
- 1/4 teaspoon salt
- 1 strawberry
- Measuring container
- Measuring spoon
- Zip-seal freezer bag
- Strainer/sieve
- Bowl
- Tall drinking glass
- Tweezers

1. Put the strawberry in a freezer bag, then pour in the water, dishwashing liquid, and salt. Remove as much air from the bag as possible, then seal it.

2. Press the bag with your fingers for at least 2 minutes to thoroughly mash up the strawberry. The soap and salt break down the fruit's cells, so that they release their DNA.

3. Press the mash through a strainer into a bowl. Then pour it from the bowl into a tall glass.

4. Ask an adult to gently drip 1 tablespoon of chilled rubbing alcohol or surgical spirits onto the surface of the strawberry liquid.

5. You will see a layer of white, stringy goop near the top of the mixture—this is strawberry DNA! Use tweezers to pull out the DNA, and take a good look at it!

Leaving a trace

DNA is not the only trace that criminals can leave at a scene. Other types of "trace evidence" include powder from their makeup, the fluff from their sweater, or soil from their boots. If a driver has crashed into another car and sped away, there may be traces of paint from their own car.

Soil is a mixture of grains of rock, dead plants and animals, water, and air. The exact mixture differs from place to place. Identifying the soil on someone's boots might tell us where they have been.

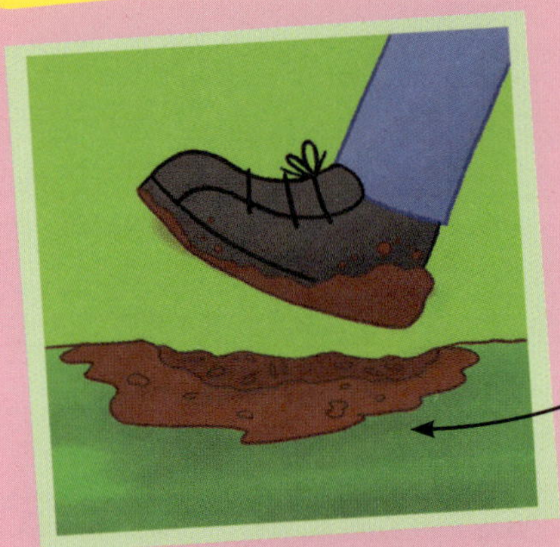

Soil can be sandy, chalky, or sticky with clay.

Soil may contain seeds or pollen from plants that grow in only one area.

Soil may be mixed with animal droppings that can be identified.

Project: Track the Trace Evidence!

Someone has broken into the Modern Art Museum and stolen a priceless masterpiece. Examine the trace evidence found at the scene of the crime, then decide which suspect to call in for questioning.

Trace Evidence Found:

- A footprint with traces of mud and red paint
- A wisp of black yarn
- A long blond hair

The Suspects:

Suspect A is a gardener and janitor.

Suspect B is a nurse.

Suspect C is a landscape painter.

Contaminated Evidence

Trace evidence must be carefully collected, stored, and tested. If not, it could become contaminated, which is when it is spoiled by contact with another material. For example, a forensic scientist might contaminate a DNA sample with their own DNA by accidentally spitting on it—which is why masks are always worn!

If a forensic scientist makes a mistake, the wrong person could be arrested—even imprisoned—for a crime. Here are 4 tips to avoid contamination:

1. Limit the number of people who enter the crime scene until the evidence has been collected.

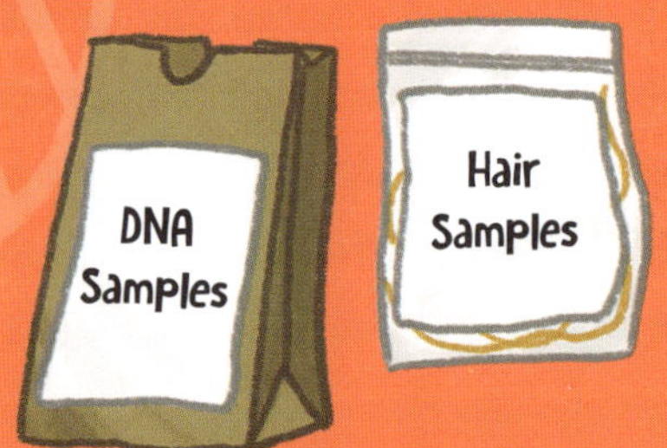

2. Everyone who visits the crime scene must wear a brand-new suit, mask, and gloves.

3. Bag and label evidence carefully.

4. Always keep the testing laboratory clean.

Project: Spot the Difference!

This crime scene has been contaminated, so it is lucky that you took a photograph when you first arrived. Spot the 5 examples of contamination.

Dental Detective

Everyone has a unique set of teeth. Teeth are different sizes and shapes. Your dentist has a record of your teeth, because they keep the X-rays that they take when checking for cavities. If someone lost their memory, it might be possible to identify them using their dental records.

Children have 20 teeth by about the age of 3. Adults have up to 32 teeth, the final "wisdom" teeth growing in at 17–21 years old. In adults, teeth wear down from a lifetime of chewing.

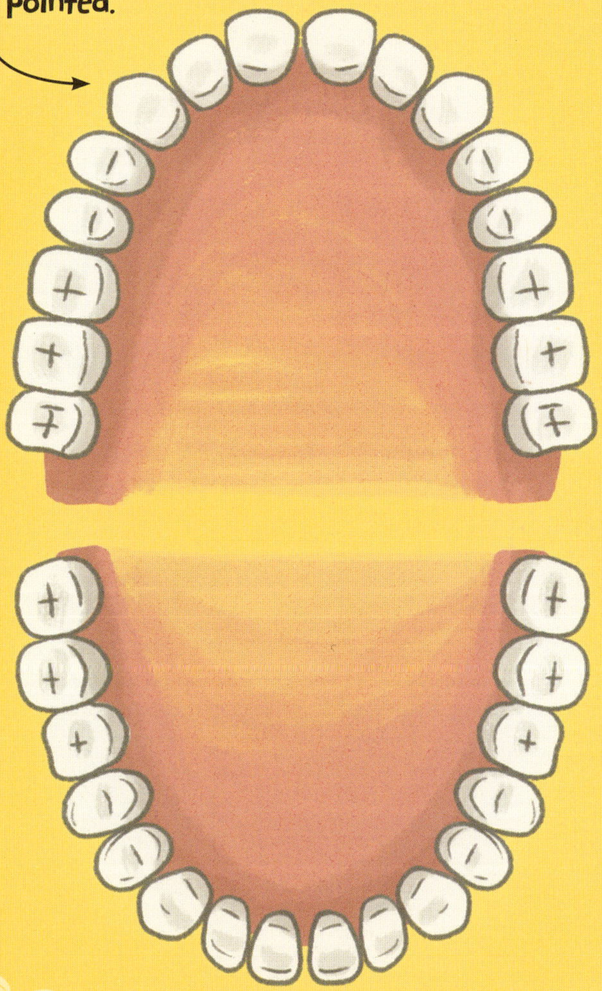

Project: Chocolate Bites!

Since everyone's teeth are slightly different, everyone leaves a different bite mark. When a thief broke into Cherry's Chocolate Shop, they made a silly mistake—they bit into a bar of chocolate and then left it behind, giving us a record of their bite. Which suspect bit the chocolate?

The Suspects:

Suspect 1

Suspect 2

Suspect 3

Suspect 4

How tall?

People with smaller feet and hands, and shorter legs and arms, are usually shorter overall. In fact, the human body usually obeys certain rules. This means that forensic scientists can make guesses about someone's height by measuring the size of their feet and the length of their steps in their footprints. They can even guess how tall a robber is by measuring how far they have reached in through an open car window ...

Project: Reaching Out!

Test out the idea that arm span is roughly equal to height.

You will need:

- A tape measure
- Pencil and paper
- A measuring partner

1. Stand with your arms straight out to the sides.

2. Ask your partner to measure from the middle figure of your left hand to the middle finger of your right hand.

3. Record the measurement.

4. Take off your shoes, then stand against a wall with your feet together and your back straight.

5. Ask your partner to hold the tape measure level with the top of your head. While they hold it in place, read off the bottom of the tape.

6. Record the measurement from step 5, then swap with your partner to take their measurements.

Is your arm span equal to your height? If not, was it less than 5 cm (2 inches) bigger or smaller than your height? Was your partner's? Do you think you have proved that arm span is roughly equal to height?

Shadow Shapes

Eyewitnesses may make confused statements. Forensic scientists understand how light and darkness affect what we think we are seeing. For example, white and yellow cars look the same under streetlights, and a dark blue or brown coat can look black in dim light.

- Opaque objects cast dark shadows because light cannot pass through them.
- Transparent objects, like clear glass and water, let light pass through them, so they do not cast a shadow.
- Translucent objects, like stained glass, block some light, casting a faint shadow.

Was one of these robbers really much taller than the other?

Project: Glass Game!

The security guard at the Glass Museum was doodling in her sketchbook when a thief tiptoed away with a priceless vase. All the guard remembers is a strange shadow crossing her page. Luckily, she sketched the shadow. Which of these suspects could have cast the shadow?

Suspect 1

Suspect 2

Suspect 3

Suspect 4

Making a Noise

Sometimes witnesses to a crime hear something—a car speeding off or glass shattering. Sounds are made when an object vibrates, shaking from side to side. This makes the surrounding air vibrate, and the vibrations travel outward as "sound waves." When the waves reach your eardrum, they make it vibrate—and you hear sounds.

Quiet sounds, like whispers, do not travel far, as the sound waves get smaller and soon disappear. Very loud sounds, like explosions, may be heard 300 km (190 miles) away.

Sound waves travel through air at 343 m (1,125 feet) per second, or roughly 20 km (12 miles) per minute.

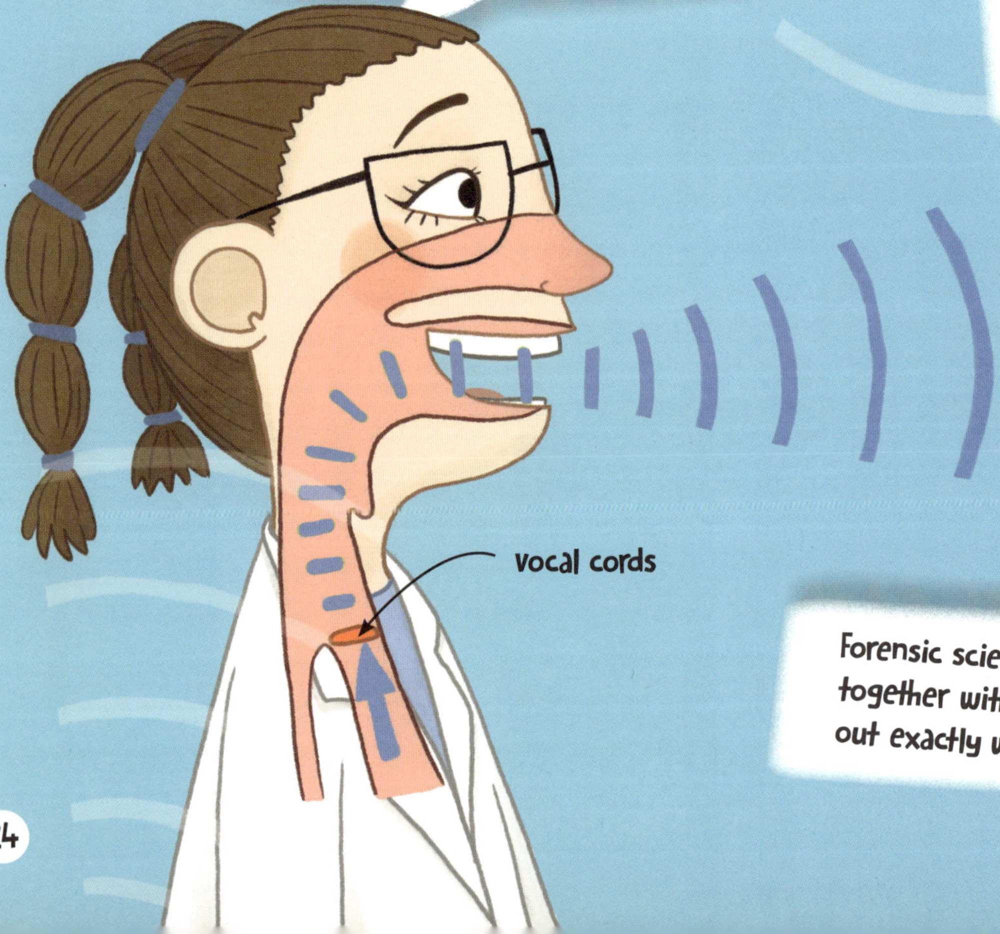

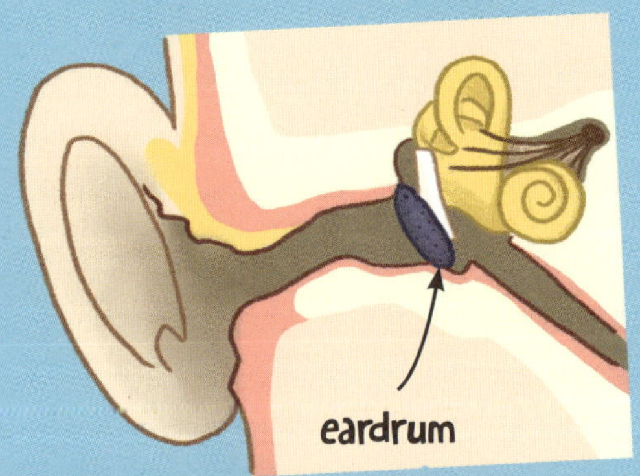

Forensic scientists can use this knowledge—together with witness statements—to work out exactly where a sound came frroum.

Project: Firework Frenzy!

Someone set off really loud fireworks at around midnight last night, waking up everyone for a long distance in every direction. The first complaint calls came in to the police station at 12.01 a.m. from point A, 12.00 a.m. from point B, and 12.02 a.m. from point C. All the callers had called immediately after hearing the first firework. Armed with the knowledge that sound travels at roughly 20 km (12 miles) per minute, mark on the map where you think the fireworks were set off.

Shatters and Splatters

A window has been smashed. The pattern of broken glass can tell you whether the window was hit from the inside or the outside, and even by what tool. Forensic scientists also study how liquids such as paint or blood behave when splattered.

If a robber breaks a window, tiny pieces of glass, less than 1 mm (0.04 inches) across, can stick in their hair and clothing. This evidence proves they made the smash!

When a window is smashed, larger fragments of glass land close to the window, mostly in the direction of the blow.

Smaller fragments can travel up to 4 m (13 feet) in all directions.

Project: Splatter Patterns

Do this experiment outdoors to avoid spoiling anything with paint. Ask an adult to cut the tops off 6 raw eggs. Empty the shells, then wash and fill each with a different shade of paint. Draw up a chart to record 6 egg drops.

You will need:

- old clothes and protective glasses
- 6 (or more) eggs
- Washable paints
- Extra-large sheets of paper
- Tape measure
- Notebook and pencil

1. You need columns for "Height of Drop," "Width of Splatter," and "Other Findings."

2. Choose a height for your first egg drop. Record the exact height in your table.

3. Drop your first egg! Record the width of the splatter and its shape. Drop the other 5 eggs from different heights.

4. Increase the height of your drops by 35 cm (1 foot) each time. To drop an egg from high up, ask an adult to use a ladder.

When the eggs are dropped, they are pulled to the ground by gravity. Gravity makes objects go faster and faster as they fall.

You should notice that the splatters get larger when the eggs are dropped from a greater height. This is because they hit the ground with greater force.

Melting Mayhem

Heat melts many materials from a solid into a liquid. Ice melts into water at 0°C (32°F), styrofoam melts at 240°C (464°F), and gold at 1,064°C (1,948°F). Could this information solve crimes? Imagine that a fire at a warehouse has melted styrofoam cups but not gold plates. This means it burned between 240°C (464°F) and 1,064°C (1,948°F)—a clue about what started it.

It is hard to believe, but metals will also turn into gas if they get really really hot. Melted gold starts evaporating into gas at around 2,800°C (5,070°F).

Water can exist in three states—solid, liquid, and gas.

At 0°C (32°F), ice melts into liquid water.

At 100°C (212°F), water boils and starts to evaporate as a gas.

Project: Ice Pop Puzzle!

It is a hot, sunny day, and someone has snatched an ice pop without paying for it. Which dripping ice pop trail leads from the ice pop stall to the thief?

Watch for Reactions

A chemical reaction happens when two materials react to each other, causing a change to both materials. For example, you create a chemical reaction when you bake a cake. The materials—including eggs and flour—change when they are mixed together and heated in the oven.

To find invisible fingerprints, scientists use an iodine spray. Iodine reacts to the oil and sweat in fingerprints, turning them bright orange.

The chemical luminol glows when it reacts to the iron in blood, which can reveal a bloodstain even if someone has wiped it up.

Forensic scientists use chemical reactions to find substances that are invisible to the naked eye.

Project: Make Invisible Ink!

Making invisible ink is a lot of fun. You can pretend you are a secret agent as you keep all your secret codes and messages hidden from others. All you need is some basic household objects and the hidden power of lemon juice.

You will need:

- Half a lemon
- Water
- Spoon
- Bowl
- Cotton swab or bud
- White paper
- Hairdryer

1. Draw a simple map of your room, using pencils, wax crayons, or marker pens.

What's going on?
Lemon juice is an organic substance that oxidizes and turns brown when heated. Diluting the lemon juice in water makes it very hard to notice when you apply it to the paper, no one will be aware of its presence until it is heated and the secret message is revealed.

2. Dip the cotton swab or bud in the lemon juice, and mark a big X where you've hidden some treasure (this can be a note for your friend or a little toy). Wait for it to dry.

3. Give the map to your friend—they won't be able to see the lemon juice mark! But gently heat the map with the hairdryer, and you'll see a brown cross emerging ...

Identify the Powder

Forensic scientists often need to identify unknown substances. That white powder may be an explosive, a poison, a drug, or just flour. To find out, take it to the lab for testing. Never touch an unknown substance with bare hands, don't taste or sniff it, and wear safety clothing to do experiments.

1. Examine the substance—using a microscope if necessary—to see if it looks like any known substances.

2. Find out if the substance chemically reacts (see page 30) to any other substances.

3. Note how the substance behaves when added to water—does it sink, float, or dissolve? Some powdery solids seem to disappear in water because they spread evenly through it. This is called dissolving.

Project: Design Your Own Experiment!

Exercise your science skills by designing your own experiment to tell apart flour, salt, and sugar. Of course, you know which is which already—but how are you going to prove it scientifically using only the listed equipment?

Your "Unknown" Substances:

- Flour
- Salt
- Sugar

You Can Use This Equipment:

- A drinking glass
- A tablespoon
- Tap water
- A clock or timer that can count in seconds
- Paper and pencil

Design a step-by-step experiment to identify the 3 substances. Consider how to measure out quantities, take timings, and record your observations.

Hint: These substances behave differently when they are added to water. One of them does not dissolve in water—it will make the water cloudy, then settle on the bottom of the glass. The two other substances dissolve in water, but one dissolves more quickly than the other.

Find the Fabric

If you are lucky, a robber will have left behind fluff from their sweater, a scrap of torn jacket on a broken window, or a snag from their socks on a fence. Forensic scientists can identify the fabric and if it matches a suspect's sweater, jacket, or socks. They come to their conclusions based on the fabric's dye, construction, and properties.

Fabric can have a range of different properties. Properties can be seen, felt, or measured.

Transparent fabrics are see-through. Opaque fabrics cannot be seen through.

Waterproof fabrics do not let water pass through them. Absorbent fabrics soak up water easily.

Strong fabrics are hard to tear. Weak fabrics are easy to rip.

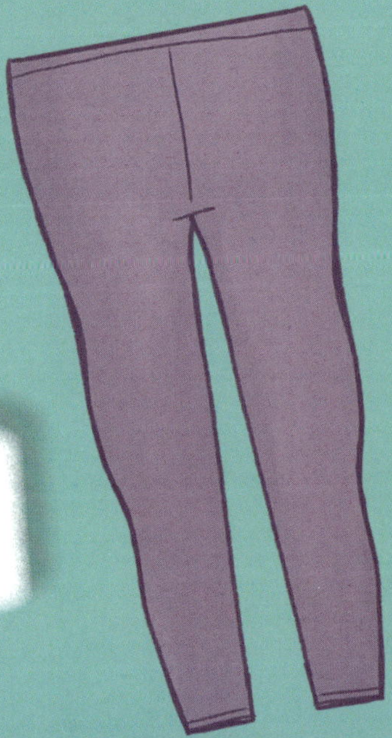

Elastic fabrics can be stretched. Rigid fabrics are hard to bend.

Project: Identify the Scrap!

While you are investigating a break-in at the swimming pool, you notice a piece of yellow fabric caught on the broken wood of the door. You take the fabric back to the laboratory for analysis. Based on the properties of the fabric, which item do you think it came from?

Properties of the Scrap:

- Opaque
- Waterproof
- Strong
- Not elastic
- Not rigid

Possible Sources of the Fabric:

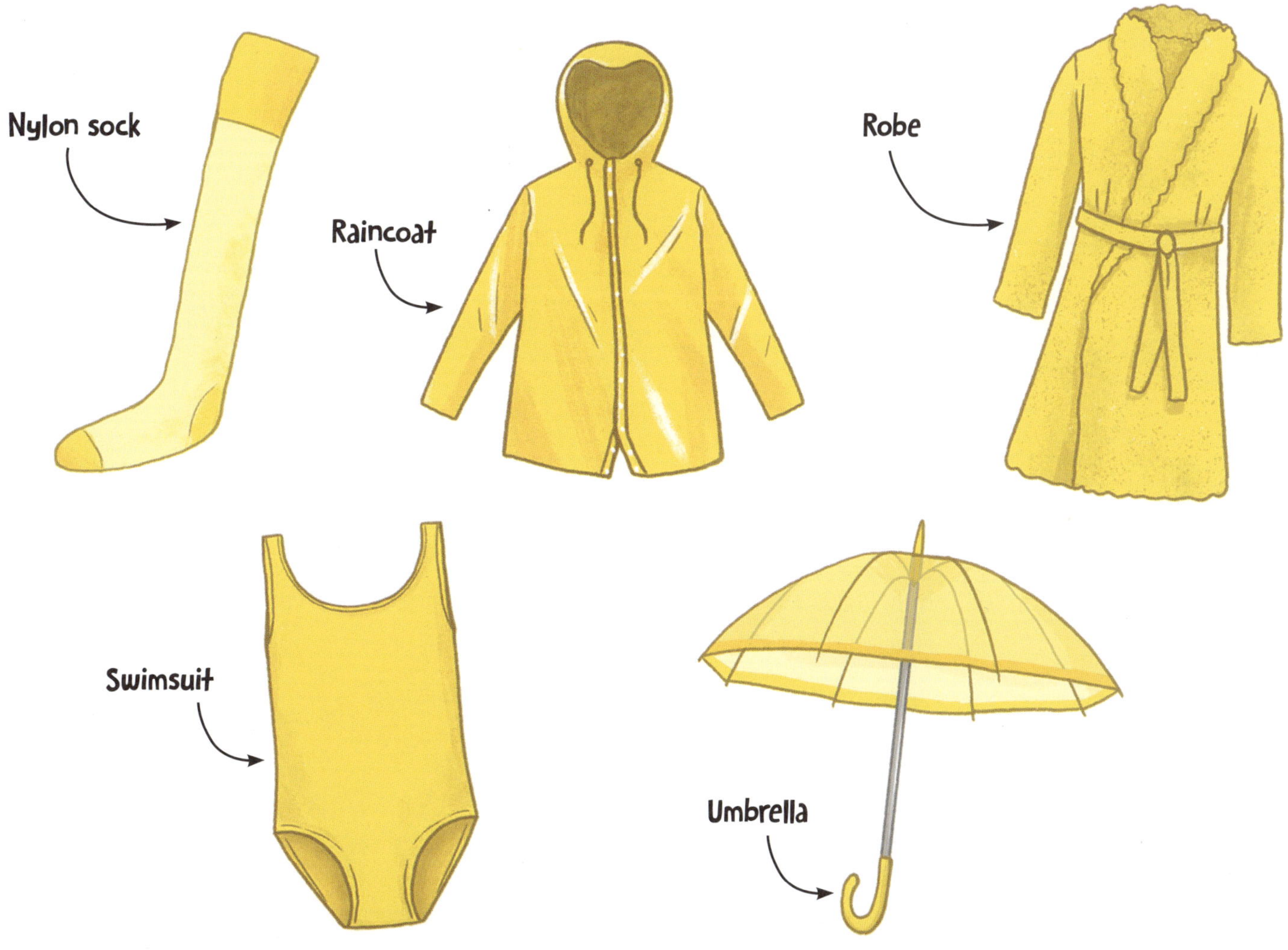

Magnetic Attraction

Everything on Earth is made of building blocks called atoms. Inside atoms are electrons that spin. Electrons spinning in one direction create an invisible force called magnetism. This happens in a small number of metals, including iron, nickel, and cobalt. These metals are attracted to magnets and can also become magnets.

A magnetic field surrounds the poles. Magnetic metals within this invisible field will be attracted or repelled.

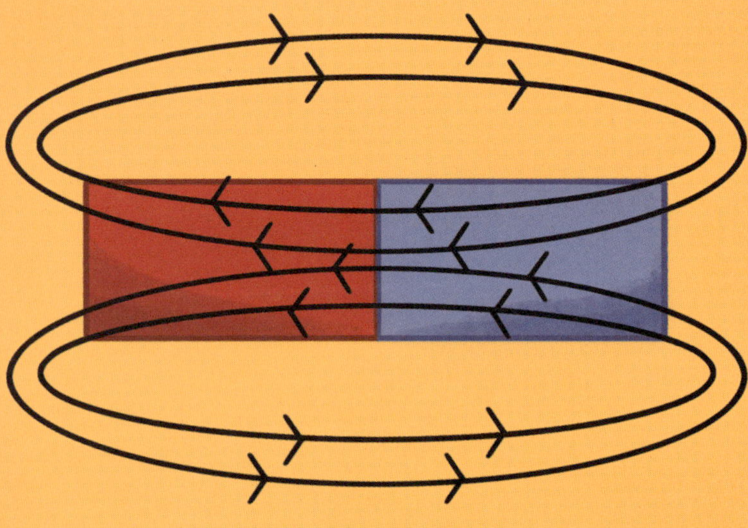

Magnets have a north pole and a south pole. The north pole of one magnet attracts the south pole and repels the north pole of another magnet.

Project: Magnet Attack!

A thief is terrorizing antique shops around the world, using a hidden magnet to steal priceless objects. Which of these objects is at risk of being stolen from Miss Ming's Antique Shop?

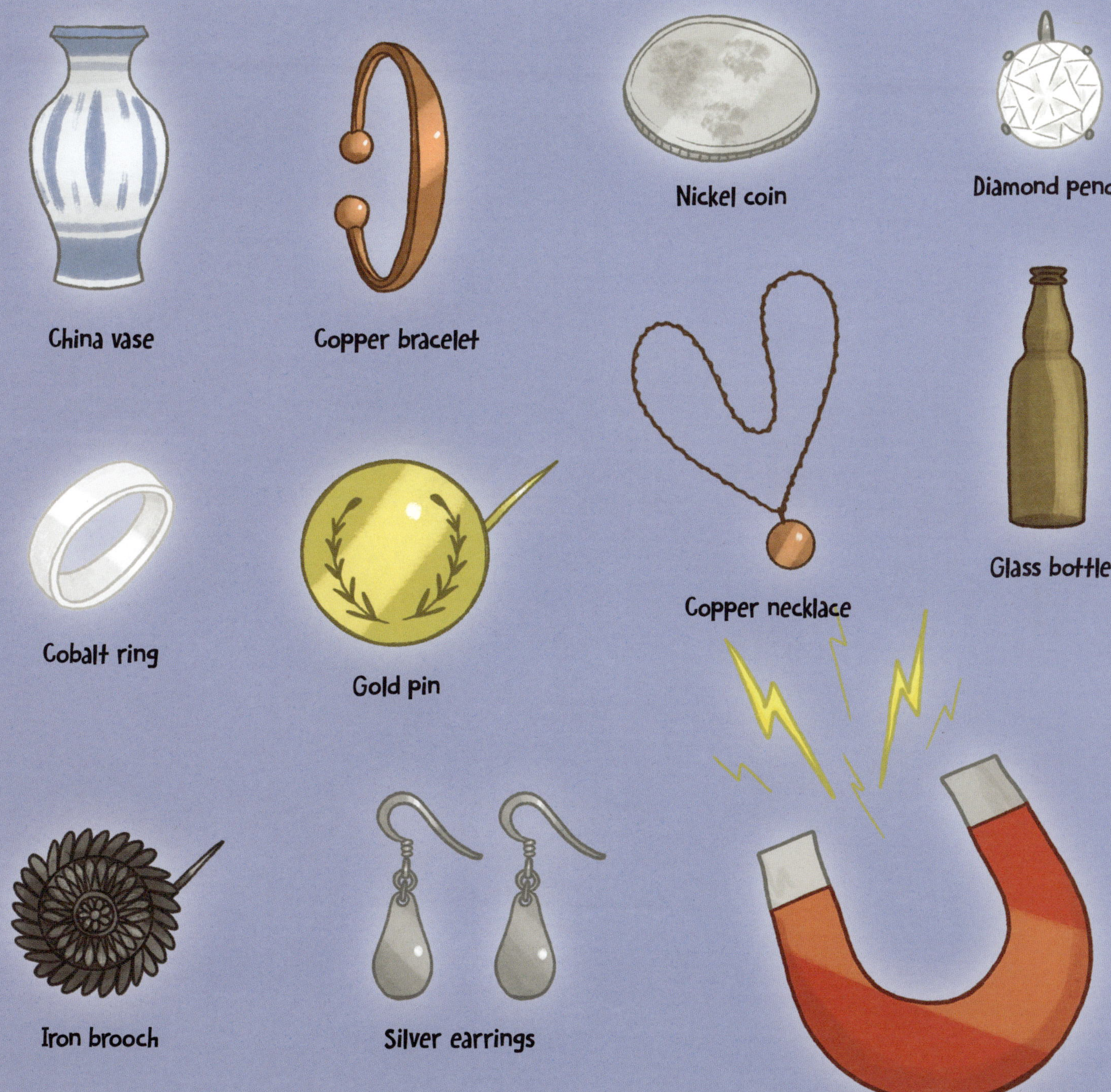

Magic Micro-Organisms

Micro-organisms are life forms like bacteria and fungi. These settle on dead animals and plants. As they feed, they grow in number. The amount of growth will tell a forensic scientist how long a substance has been lying around.

These micro-organisms do a vital job. As they feed, they help to break down dead plants, animals, and waste. If nothing decayed, the planet would be piled high with garbage!

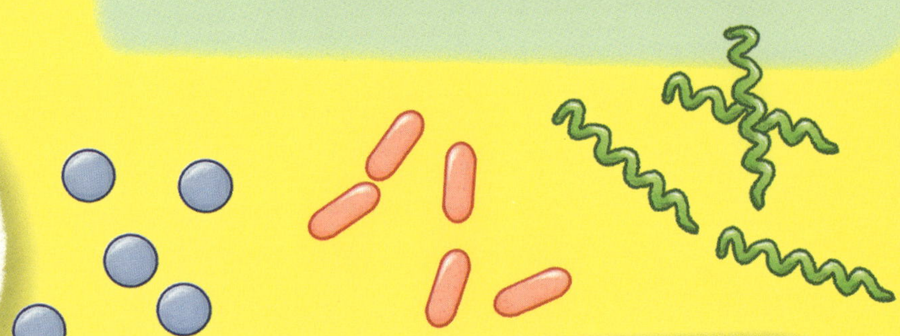

Bacteria are in three main shapes—spirals, rods, and spheres. Thousands of bacteria could fit on the dot at the end of this sentence.

Fungi range from tiny micro-organisms to large mushrooms and toadstools.

Project: Grow Fungi!

To study the growth of micro-organisms, try this experiment to grow fungi on bread. Fungi spores are like the seeds of a fungus. Spores are all around us, so they will land on the bread without your help.

You will need:

- 3 slices of bread
- A bowl of water
- 3 zip-seal freezer bags
- Paper and pencil

1. Dunk each slice of bread in the water. Put each slice in its own zip-seal freezer bag, then seal the bag tightly.

2. Put the first bag in the freezer; the second in a warm spot, such as by a radiator; and the third at "room temperature."

3. Without opening the bags, check on the growth of micro-organisms on the bread after 5, 7, and 10 days. Write down your observations, as well as predictions about future growth.

4. Throw away the bags without opening them!

Once you have sealed the bags, do not reopen them, because you will release fungi spores into the air. This could make you unwell, particularly if you have allergies.

Spreading Infection

Some micro-organisms cause illness in humans. Viruses cause infectious diseases that pass from person to person, such as chicken pox. Some bacteria cause illness such as stomach upsets from eating dirty food. Some forensic scientists are experts on disease-causing micro-organisms and can tell when an outbreak began.

More than 200 different viruses cause colds.

Cold viruses travel from an infected person in coughs and sneezes or in snot wiped onto objects.

For 1 to 3 days, the "incubation period," the infected person has no symptoms, although the virus has invaded the cells in their nose, mouth, and throat.

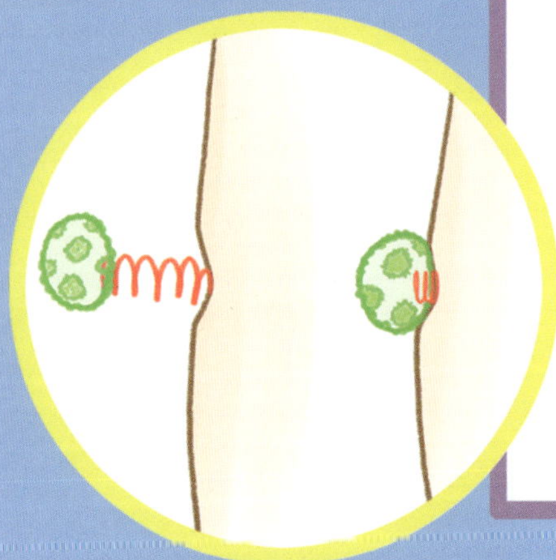

The infected person's body fights back. Symptoms appear—sore throat, runny nose, coughing, headache, and fever—and may last 7–10 days.

Project: Who Spread the Infection?

A burglar broke into the Infectious Disease Laboratory, breaking a vial containing the Green Spot virus and infecting themselves immediately. Seven days after the break-in, three suspects have arrived at the police station for questioning. Which suspect could have committed the burglary?

Facts about the Green Spot Virus:

- Incubation period is 3 days.
- The only symptom is large green spots.
- Spots last 5 days.
- The sufferer is highly infectious as soon as the spots appear.

The Suspects:

Suspect A
Seven days after the break-in, Suspect A has no spots, and neither do her family and friends.

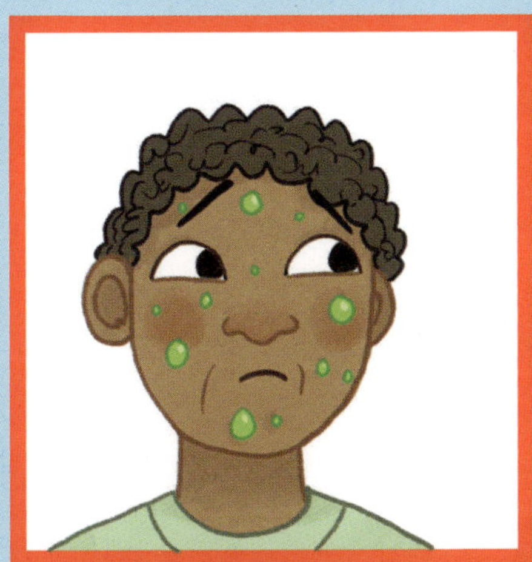

Suspect B
Seven days after the break-in, Suspect B has green spots, but his family and friends do not.

Suspect C
Seven days after the break-in, Suspect C has green spots and so do her family and friends.

Analyzing Handwriting

Strange as it seems, some criminals may write a letter to a newspaper or the police. Handwriting experts try to match the handwriting to samples of writing from suspects. Experts might also be called in when someone is suspected of forging someone else's signature on a document.

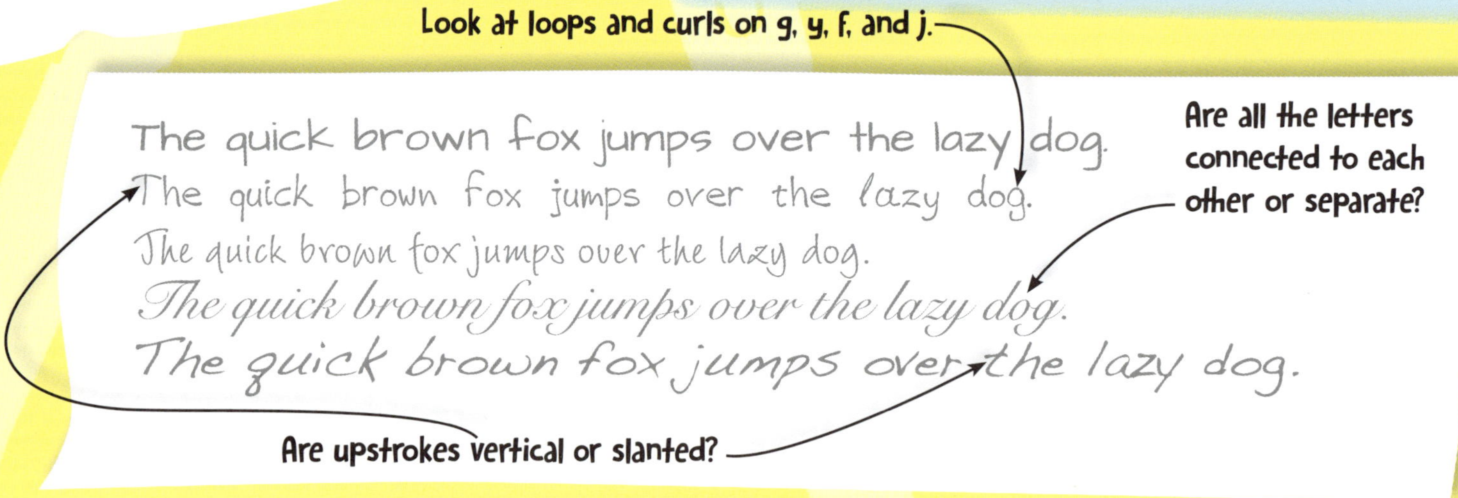

Handwriting experts look at these key points:

1. The ways the letters are formed—everyone writes each letter a little differently.
2. The style of writing—the way handwriting is taught has changed over the years and differs from region to region.
3. The smoothness and darkness of the lines show how hard the writer presses and how fast they write.
4. Signs that the writer is disguising their handwriting. Shaky starts and lots of pen lifts reveal they are writing slowly and possibly copying.

Project: Match the Handwriting!

A bicycle thief left a rude note for the bike's owner. Handwriting samples have been supplied by three suspects. Who wrote the note?

Note Left at the Crime Scene:

I stole your bike!
Ha ha!

Handwriting Samples from Suspects:

Suspect A I stole your bike!

Suspect B I stole your bike!

Suspect C I stole your bike!

No two samples of handwriting from one person will be completely identical! Look for similarities between samples, but also watch out for differences that could rule out any suspects.

Ink Test

Another way to find out who wrote a note is to match its ink with the ink in a suspect's pen. The method for doing this is called chromatography. Ink is a mixture of different pigments, or shades. Chromatography separates the pigments so we can see them. The method can also match the dye in a scrap of cloth with the dye in a suspect's clothing.

Banks may protect their money with packets of dye, which are exploded by remote control if the money is stolen. Chromatography matches the dye on a suspect's hands and face with the bank's dye.

Even black inks are mixtures of different pigments.

Project: Separate the Inks!

Have a go at chromatography for yourself. When the water is absorbed by the paper towel, the pigments dissolve in the water. Some molecules of pigments are smaller and lighter than others, so they travel farther up the paper. That is why the pigments separate. Try to predict which pigments each ink will split into.

You will need:

- Paper towel
- Water
- 4 drinking glasses
- Washable marker pens in black, red, blue, and green

1. Cut the paper towel into 4 strips about 5 cm (2 inches) wide and around 25 cm (10 inches) long. Pour about 0.5 cm (1/4 inch) of water into each glass.

2. On each strip of paper towel, make a large spot with a different marker pen, about 2.5 cm (1 inch) from the bottom.

3. Place the spotted end of each strip in a glass, making sure the spot does not go in the water. Fold over the top of the towel to keep it from slipping.

4. Watch as the water is absorbed by the towel, splitting the ink as it travels up the paper. Let the strips dry, and then examine the pigments.

Computer Crime

The police can solve crimes from information on computers and phones, such as emails, text messages, and files—even deleted files. The time of a text message or email could prove where a suspect was. The content of a message could prove that a criminal mastermind gave the order to rob a bank!

The letters at the end of a computer file's name are called "filename extensions." They give clues about what sort of file it is:

Files names that end in .mp3 contain sounds, such as songs.

File names that end in .jpeg are usually photos.

File names that end in .doc or .docx contain mostly words.

Did you know that whenever you look at a website, it leaves a record on your computer or phone? So don't look at a website called www.getawaydrivers.com if you are planning to rob a bank!

File names that end in .xls contain tables and charts.

Project: File Forensics!

A bank has been robbed, and a suspect has been arrested for the crime. Examine the list of files found on their computer. Find 3 files that may contain evidence.

List of Files:

- birthdayparty.jpeg
- cutedog.jpeg
- happybirthday.mp3
- fluffykitten.jpeg
- funnykitten.jpeg
- hairydog.jpeg
- howtocrackasafe.doc
- jinglebells.mp3
- lonesomeblues.mp3
- mewithfriend.jpeg
- naughtykitten.jpeg
- newyorkbank.jpeg
- prettyflower.jpeg
- robberyschedule.xls
- christmaslist.doc
- seaside.jpeg
- wewishyouamerrychristmas.mp3

Phone Finder

When you make a call on your smartphone, it sends your words through the air as radio waves. These are picked up by a nearby phone tower, which can send and receive radio waves over large distances. A network of towers sends your radio waves to the phone of the person you are talking with.

Information from phone towers can reveal not just where someone made a call but also whether they were on the move.

The caller was in one spot for the whole call.

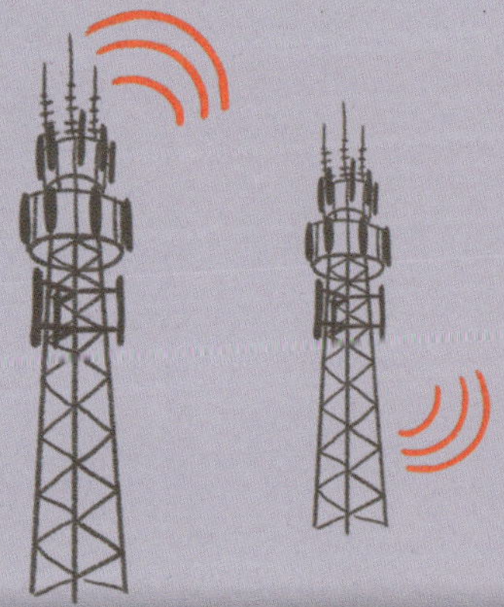

The caller moved past several phone towers while they talked.

Project: Find the Injured Hiker!

A hiker has called Mountain Rescue to say that he has twisted his ankle somewhere along a remote mountain track. Using information from the local phone towers, we have discovered that his phone is 8 km (5 miles) from phone tower A and 16 km (10 miles) from phone tower B. Use this map of the track and a ruler to find out where the injured hiker is.

A Worthy Witness?

When there are witnesses to a crime, it is important to make a careful note of their memories. Try to judge what is true or untrue, what is important, and what is not. Witnesses can forget details, get confused, or be influenced by others.

If you remembered everything that ever happened, your brain would overload! Your brain selects what you need to remember and how long to remember it for.

Some memories are not needed for long (like remembering to put your snack in your bag). The brain stores these at the front of the head for a short time, then forgets them!

Some things seem unimportant (like the number of windows in the house you just walked past), so they are not remembered at all.

Some memories are stored forever, all around the brain. These long-term memories are useful (such as how to read) or important to us (such as very happy or sad events).

Project: Witness Statement!

How good a witness do you think you would be? How strong do you think your long-term and short-term memories are? Try this exercise to find out more.

Write down what you did yesterday for each hour of the day.

Now write down what you did four weeks ago on Saturday.

What have you learned about your memory? Were some things easier to remember than others? Did you have to make guesses?

Assessing Alibis

An alibi is a claim that a suspect was in a different place when a crime was committed, proving that they could not have done it. An excellent alibi would be giving a speech in front of an audience at exactly the time a crime took place! Most alibis need to be investigated.

Look for other people to corroborate, or back up, a suspect's alibi. Hunt for evidence, such as movie tickets or images from security cameras, which proves a suspect was where they claim to have been.

You may need to do calculations to check alibis. For example: A suspect owns a car with a maximum speed of 80 km/h (50 mph). They were definitely in Smalltown at 9 a.m. A crime took place 160 km (100 miles) away in Bigtown at 10 a.m. Could the suspect have reached Bigtown in time to commit the crime? The answer is no! Driving at 80 km/h (50 mph), it would have taken the suspect 2 hours to travel 160 km (100 miles), reaching Bigtown no earlier than 11 a.m.

Project: Check that Alibi!

Someone stole all the bananas from the supermarket in Bluetown at 4 p.m. yesterday afternoon. Read these statements given by three possible suspects, then figure out who does not have an alibi.

Suspect A

Yesterday afternoon, I walked my dog Charlie in Bluetown Park. There, I bumped into my friend Beth, who was walking her dog Pepper, at around 3 p.m. Then I drove to Main Street in Redtown to watch a movie, which finished at 5.30 p.m. I dropped off Charlie at my friend Carla's house just before the movie started. Luckily, Carla lives right on Main Street.

Suspect B

Yesterday evening, I was playing Dorothy in Bluetown's performance of *The Wizard of Oz*. The show started at 7 p.m. I went to the supermarket at around 3.45 p.m. to pick up cookies for the cast before our rehearsal, which began at 4.15 p.m. After picking up the cookies, I drove to Fiona's Flowers over in Yellowtown, about 20 km (12 miles) away, to buy flowers for our director, Viv.

Suspect C

Yesterday afternoon, I walked my poodle Pepper in Bluetown Park. I bumped into my friend Emma there, who was walking her dog Charlie. After saying goodbye to Emma, I drank some lemonade in the park café. I probably stayed in the café for about 30 minutes, chatting with the café owner. A bit later, I went to see a performance of *The Wizard of Oz*, which my friend Viv directed.

Detecting Lies

In some countries, including the United States, "lie detector" machines are used to try to tell if a suspect is lying. They test for signs of nervousness, such as a fast heartbeat. Unfortunately, innocent people can get nervous, and guilty people who are used to telling lies can pass them!

When we feel nervous or afraid, the brain releases hormones that give us a burst of energy, so we can run away from or fight the danger. Here are some signs that those hormones have been released:

1. Faster heartbeat.
2. Faster breathing.
3. Quicker blinking.
4. Blushing and sweating.
5. Pursed lips because of a dry mouth.

Never believe that a suspect is guilty until you have collected and tested evidence—and, most importantly, before they have received a trial in a court of law.

Project: Take Your Pulse!

Your heart is a muscle that pumps blood around your body by squeezing. Every time the heart squeezes, it sends a wave, or pulse, of blood through your veins. You can feel this pulse most easily where a vein passes over a bone, such as at your wrist. Try this experiment to see the effect of exercise on your pulse.

You will need:

- A stopwatch
- Paper and pencil
- A partner

1. To find the pulse on your wrist, place two fingers at the base of your thumb, then slide your fingers straight down onto your wrist. Press gently until you feel a faint, throbbing pulse.

2. Ask your partner to start the stopwatch. Count how many times you feel your pulse in 1 minute. Your partner should say "Stop" when the minute is up.

3. Now run on the spot for 1 minute.

4. As soon as you stop jumping, ask your partner to start the stopwatch. Count how many times you feel your pulse in 1 minute.

5. Compare the two heart rates. What do you notice?

Get to Work!

Forensic science is always improving. In ancient times, science was hardly ever used to solve crimes because people knew little about the human body, materials, or forces. Slowly, and particularly in the last 150 years, scientists have developed new tests and tools to solve crimes.

> If you would like to be a forensic scientist, pay attention in science at school, train yourself to notice details and to take careful notes, and always be honest and fair.

Did you know these forensic science records?

In 1888, photographs were first used to record the details of crime scenes.

The first crime was solved using fingerprint evidence in 1892.

In 1910, the first police laboratory was set up for examining trace evidence.

In 1984, the first police department was set up to solve crimes using computer evidence.

DNA evidence was first used to solve a crime in 1987.

Project: First Steps!

Now that you are a forensic scientist, you have arrived at your first crime scene. You should take the following steps, but in what order?

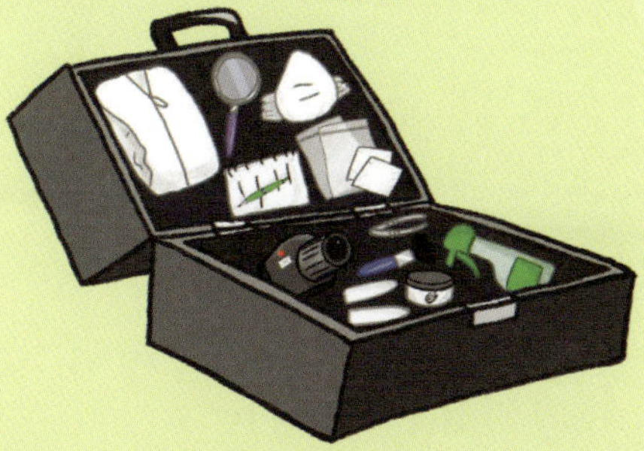

A Put evidence in clean bags or boxes, then seal and label them. Write your name on the seals so no one can open the evidence without you noticing.

B Without disturbing anything, survey the crime scene. Decide what types of evidence may be present and how to collect them.

C Search for trace and DNA evidence.

D Photograph the scene, making sure your photos show the location of every piece of evidence you have found. Make careful notes about all the details.

E Put on clean gloves, mask, and suit. Seal off the crime scene with police tape, so that no one can enter without permission.

F Make sure that the sealed evidence is taken to the police laboratory by yourself or a trusted officer. Keep a record of every bag and box.

G Ask the police officer who has taken charge of the crime scene for information.

Pop Quiz

Have you been paying attention? Try answering these questions to test all of your newly acquired forensic knowledge

1. Is this a loop or a whorl fingerprint pattern?

2. True or false? Your DNA is the same as your mother's, and different to your cousin.

3. List three different types of trace evidence that you might look for at a crime scene.

4. Why do forensic scientists wear masks, gloves, protective suits, and shoe covers? Is it:

   A) So that police officers can easily identify forensic scientists.

   B) So that they don't get their own clothes dirty.

   C) Because it's important that the scientists can't contaminate the scene with anything from their own bodies, clothes, or shoes.

5. How fast do sound waves travel through the air?

   A) 34 m/second (111 ft/second)

   B) 343 m/second (1,125 ft/second)

   C) 3,434 m/second (2 miles/second)

6. Try to guess from the filename alone which of these is likely to be a song, which is likely to be a picture, and which is likely to be a text file:

   shopping.doc
   holidays.jpg
   mynumberone.mp3

7. **Which 5 of these signs <u>might</u> indicate that a suspect is telling a lie?**

faster heartbeat
eye-rolling
dribbling
pursed lips
slower blinking
faster breathing
sneezing
blushing or sweating
faster blinking
hiccups

8. **True or false: Witnesses always agree on the facts—if there are differences in their accounts, it means that one of them is lying.**

9. **How many teeth does an adult human usually have?**

A) 32
B) 36
C) 40

10. **If you found a pen that you thought a suspect had used, what might you look for to confirm your suspicions—fingerprints or DNA?**

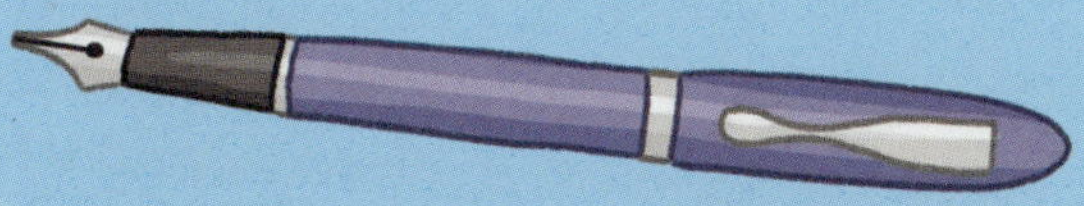

Write down your answers here, and check them on page 61.

1 ....

2 ....

3 ....

4 ....

5 ....

6 ....

7 ....

8 ....

9 ....

10 ....

Answers

P. 5 Bag 3 contains all the necessary items.

P. 9 Suspect 4: Percy the Pig ate all the cookies.

P. 11

P. 15 It may be worth calling in Suspect C for questioning.

P. 17

P. 19 Suspect C bit into the chocolate.

P. 23 Suspect 3 could have cast the shadow.

P. 25 The fireworks were set off somewhere near point B.

P. 29

P. 33 Drop one tablespoon of each substance into a fresh glass of water. Start a timer when the substance enters the water. Stir continuously to try to dissolve the substance. The tablespoon of flour will not dissolve. When you stop stirring, it will sink to the bottom of the glass. The tablespoon of sugar will dissolve faster than the salt. The greater the quantity of sugar and salt, the longer they will take to dissolve and the greater the time difference between them.

P. 35 The fabric was ripped from the raincoat.

P. 37 The iron brooch, nickel coin, and cobalt ring are made from magnetic metals and are at risk of being stolen.

P. 41 Based on the symptoms of Suspect C and her family and friends, she could have carried out the break-in.

P. 43 Suspect B wrote the note.

P. 47 The files howtocrackasafe.doc, newyorkbank.jpeg, and robberyschedule.xls may be worth examining.

P. 49

P. 53 Suspect A was probably dropping off her dog at Carla's house in Redtown at 4 p.m. Check with Carla that this alibi is true. Suspect B was probably buying flowers in Yellowtown at 4 p.m. Check with Fiona's Flowers to make sure. Suspect C has no alibi for 4 p.m. Suspect C met Suspect A and her dog Charlie in Bluetown Park at around 3 p.m., then spent half an hour in the park café. We do not know where she was between 3.30 p.m. and 7 p.m., when the performance of *The Wizard of Oz* began.

P. 57 The correct order of steps is: G E B C D A F.

P. 59

1. It is a whorl fingerprint pattern.
2. False. You get half of your DNA from your biological mother and half from your biological father, so no other person in the world has exactly the same DNA as you (unless you're an identical twin!).
3. You might look for some of the following:
   - footprints
   - fingerprints
   - body fluids
   - hair
   - soil/dirt
   - paint
   - broken glass
   - tiny pieces of clothes.
4. C.
5. B.
6. shopping.doc is likely to be a text file.
   holidays.jpg is likely to be a picture.
   mynumberone.mp3 is likly to be a song.
7. faster heartbeat
   pursed lips
   faster breathing
   blushing or sweating
   faster blinking
8. False. People often remember things slightly differently, so differences don't necessarily mean that someone is deliberately lying.
9. A.
10. Both! You might also want to compare the ink on the note to the ink in the pen to see if they match.

Glossary

Alibi Evidence showing that a person was somewhere else when a crime was committed.

Analysis Careful examination of something in order to understand it.

Bacteria Micro-organisms with just one cell; some can cause illness in humans.

Body fluids Liquids made in the human body, including blood and tears.

Cell A tiny building block from which living things are made. All living things are either single cells or are made from many cells working together.

Chemical reaction A change that takes place when two or more substances combine to form a new substance.

Chromatography A method of separating a mixture into its different parts.

Corroborate To confirm or support something, such as an idea or statement.

Decay To rot or decompose through the action of bacteria and fungi.

Dissolve When a solid is mixed into a liquid and becomes part of it.

DNA (deoxyribonucleic acid) The material found in the cells of nearly all living things that controls the growth and work of cells. The instructions contained in DNA are passed down from parents to their children.

Eardrum A thin skin within each ear that moves backward and forward very quickly when reached by sound waves.

Evaporate To change from a liquid into a gas.

Evidence Information or materials that prove whether or not something is true. Evidence can be used in a court of law to try to prove the facts about a crime.

Eyewitnesses People who saw a crime happen.

Forensic scientists Experts who use scientific methods to collect and test evidence in order to solve crimes. Science is the study of natural things through careful looking and experimenting.

Forging Making a copy of something in order to deceive, or trick.

Fungi Living things that get their food from rotting material or other living things.

Decode Convert a coded message into an understandable one.

Density The weight of an object compared to the amount of space it fills.

Diameter The distance of a straight line from side to side passing through the midpoint of a circle.

Gravity A force that pulls all objects toward each other. The larger the object, the greater

the pull of its gravity, so Earth's gravity is much greater than a child's.

Incubation period The time between being exposed to an infection and getting the first symptoms.

Iodine A purplish chemical that is found naturally on Earth.

Laboratory A room or building set up for scientific experiments and research.

Liquid A substance that flows, such as water, milk, or vinegar.

Luminol A man-made chemical that can be made to glow bright blue through chemical reactions.

Micro-organisms Living things too small to be seen without the help of a microscope.

Microscope An instrument that uses lenses to view very small objects and living things.

Molecule A group of atoms that are joined to each other.

Nucleus The "brain" of a cell that helps control its function, including growth and reproduction. It contains a person's hereditary information from their parents.

Opaque Not able to be seen through.

Pigment A substance that gives black, white, or another shade to materials.

Pollen A powder made by the male parts of a flower. When the female parts of a flower receive pollen, they can produce seeds.

Properties The qualities of matter that can be seen, felt, or measured.

Radio waves Invisible energy that can travel through the air. Radio waves are often used for sending communications, such as radio and television shows or phone conversations.

Sample A small part of a substance, often used for testing.

Solid Firm and keeping a distinct shape.

Sound waves Patterns of vibration, or shaking, that travel outward from the source of a sound.

Spores Cells produced by fungi, bacteria, and some other living things that can grow into new fungi or bacteria.

Suspect A person thought to be possibly guilty of a crime.

Symptoms Changes in the body and brain caused by a disease.

Trace evidence Materials left behind while committing a crime, including hair, scraps or threads of clothing, soil, and glass.

Translucent Able to be seen through, but objects on the other side look unclear.

Transparent Able to be seen through, so that objects on the other side are clear.

Unique Unlike anything else.

Vibrate To move quickly to and fro.

Viruses Micro-organisms that can only reproduce (by making copies of themselves) inside the cells of other living things. Viruses can cause illness.

Index

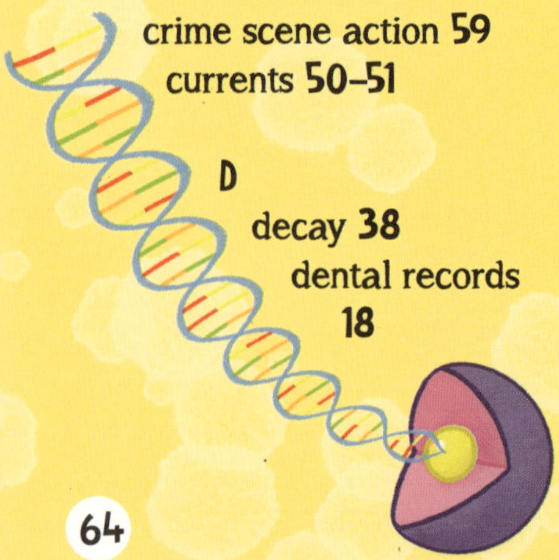

Klasse! neu 1

Noch mal!

Corinna Schicker
Morag McCrorie

Arbeitsheft

Name: ....

Klasse: ....

OXFORD

OXFORD
UNIVERSITY PRESS

Great Clarendon Street, Oxford OX2 6DP

Oxford University Press is a department of the University of Oxford. It furthers the University's objective of excellence in research, scholarship, and education by publishing worldwide in

Oxford New York

Auckland Cape Town Dar es Salaam Hong Kong Karachi Kuala Lumpur Madrid Melbourne Mexico City Nairobi New Delhi Shanghai Taipei Toronto

With offices in

Argentina Austria Brazil Chile Czech Republic France Greece Guatemala Hungary Italy Japan Poland Portugal Singapore South Korea Switzerland Thailand Turkey Ukraine Vietnam

Oxford is a registered trade mark of Oxford University Press in the UK and in certain other countries

First published 2005

British Library Cataloguing in Publication Data

Data available

ISBN-13: 978-0-19-840646-4
ISBN-10: 0-19-840646-0

10 9 8 7 6 5 4 3 2 1

Printed in Spain by Unigraf.

Acknowledgements

Illustrations are by: Martin Aston **pp4, 13, 31, 73**; Phil Burrows **pp5, 9, 14, 18, 22, 27t, 33, 34b, 35, 36, 41, 42, 51, 52, 74**; Stefan Chabluk **pp24, 32t, 34t, 56, 58, 60, 63t&br, 64, 65t, 71, 72**; Doreen Lang **pp15, 23, 27b, 32, 47, 49, 55, 57, 59, 63bl, 65bl, 66, 67, 76**; Mike Miller: **pp39, 40, 42b, 43, 50b, 65b, 66**; David Mostyn **p50t**; Bill Piggins **p8**.

Inhalt

1.1 Wie geht's?

1 **Finde die Wörter. Schreib die Wörter auf.**
Find the words and write them down.

HALLOGUTENTAGAUFWIEDERSEHENGUTENACHTTSCHÜSGUTENMORGEN

Hallo

2 **Schreib Antworten.**
Write answers.

a Hallo! — Guten Tag!

b Guten Morgen!

c Guten Abend!

d Tschüs!

3 **Was sagen sie?**
Find the correct words for each picture.

Prima!
Nicht so gut.
Schlecht!
Danke, gut!

Wie heißt du?

1 **Was sagen sie? Füll die Sprechblasen aus.**
What are they saying? Fill in the speech bubbles with the phrases from the box.

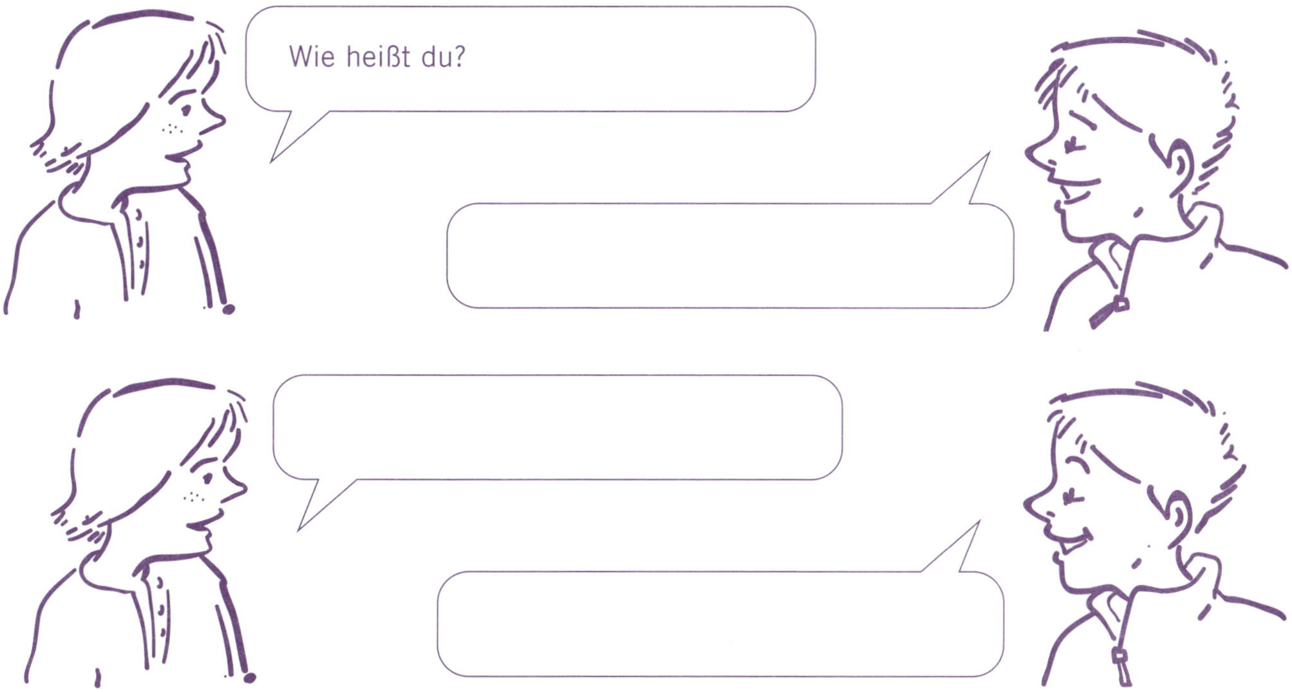

Ich heiße Stefan.	Wie schreibt man das?	S –T – E – F – A – N.

2 **Schreib die Namen in der richtigen Alphabet-Reihenfolge auf.**
Write down the names alphabetically.

Uwe   Hannah   Philipp   Stefan   Thomas   Wilhelm
Monika   Julia   Daniel   Florian   Anne   Benjamin

a ______________________ g ______________________
b ______________________ h ______________________
c ______________________ i ______________________
d ______________________ j ______________________
e ______________________ k ______________________
f ______________________ l ______________________

1.3 Wie alt bist du?

1 **Finde acht Zahlen.**
Find eight numbers.

F	G	H	S	I	E	B	E	N	P
F	Ü	N	F	Z	E	H	N	X	R
E	I	N	S	C	Z	W	Ö	L	F
D	A	Q	S	E	C	H	S	L	P
M	Z	W	A	N	Z	I	G	T	W
T	S	I	E	B	Z	E	H	N	L
J	U	L	F	Z	E	H	N	D	B

Beispiel: 1 6 ~~7~~ 10 12 15 17 20

2 **Schreib die Zahlen auf.**
Write down the numbers.

12 ____________ 2 ____________ 7 ____________

15 ____________ 6 ____________ 3 ____________

4 ____________ 20 ____________ 17 ____________

3 **„Wie alt bist du?" Schreib Sätze.**
Write sentences with the information.

Beispiel: *10 – Ich bin zehn Jahre alt.*

a 14 **b** 12 **c** 16 **d** 11 **e** 13 **f** 15

a ____________ **d** ____________

b ____________ **e** ____________

c ____________ **f** ____________

Wann hast du Geburtstag?

1 Finde die Wörter.

Write down the months of the year.

RILAP	ARNUJA	TEMSEPBER
a April	b ______	c ______
LIJU	**NOBERVEM**	**BERDEZEM**
d ______	e ______	f ______
USTAUG	**IAM**	**TOOKBER**
g ______	h ______	i ______
ARFEBRU	**ZÄRM**	**NIUJ**
j ______	k ______	l ______

2 Was passt? Schreib die passenden Wörter auf.

Write down the months for the seasons.

Mein Klassenzimmer

1 **Finde die Wörter. Schreib die Wörter auf.**
Find the words and write them down.

a	eine Schü	zimmer	**a**	eine Schülerin
b	ein Klassen	tisch	**b**	
c	ein St	er	**c**	
d	eine Ta	lerin	**d**	
e	ein Schreib	fel	**e**	
f	ein Lehr	uhl	**f**	

2 **Was ist das? Schreib die Wörter auf.**
Write down the words for a–h.

a ein Lehrer

b ______

c ______

d ______

e ______

f ______

g ______

h ______

Grammatik 1

Flashback

ich = *I* du = *you*

1 **Finde die passenden Verben für die Sätze.**
Underline the correct verb for each sentence.

a Wann hast / habe du Geburtstag?

b Ich heißt / heiße Markus.

c Ich bin / bist 14 Jahre alt.

d Wie heiße / heißt du?

e Ich habe / hat im Juni Geburtstag.

f Wie alt bin / bist du?

2 **Füll die Lücken aus.**
Fill in the gaps with the correct verbs.

a

b

c

Grammatik 2

Flashback

Maskulinum	der/ein Schüler	=	*the/a male pupil*
Femininum	die/eine Lehrerin	=	*the/a female teacher*
Neutrum	das/ein Klassenzimmer	=	*the/a classroom*

1 Unterstreiche alle Maskulin-Wörter in Blau, alle Feminin-Wörter in Rot und alle Neutrum-Wörter in Grün.
Underline all masculine words in blue, all feminine words in red and all neuter words in green.

a ein Stuhl　　b die Tafel　　c das Fenster

d eine Schülerin　　e der Lehrer　　f das Klassenzimmer

g ein Schreibtisch　　h die Tür　　i ein Schüler

j eine Wand　　k eine Lehrerin　　l das Buch

2 Schreib die Wörter in Übung 1 mit *der/die/das* oder *eine/ein/ein* auf.
Write down the words in activity 1 with der/die/das *or* ein/eine/ein.

Beispiel:

a der Stuhl ______　　b ______

c ______　　d ______

e ______　　f ______

g ______　　h ______

i ______　　j ______

k ______　　l ______

Vokabular

Guten Tag sagen	***Greetings***
Hallo!	*Hello!*
Guten Morgen!	*Good morning!*
Guten Tag!	*Good day!*
Guten Abend!	*Good evening!*
Gute Nacht!	*Good night!*
Tschüs!	*Bye!*
Auf Wiedersehen!	*Goodbye!*
Wie geht's?	*How are you?*
Danke, sehr gut.	*Very well, thanks.*
Prima.	*Great.*
Gut.	*Fine.*
Nicht so gut.	*Not so good.*
Schlecht.	*Awful/Not very well.*
Wie heißt du?	*What's your name?*
Ich heiße Melanie.	*I am called Melanie.*

Geburtstage	***Birthdays***
Wie alt bist du?	*How old are you?*
Ich bin 13 Jahre alt.	*I am thirteen years old.*
eins	*1*
zwei	*2*
drei	*3*
vier	*4*
fünf	*5*
sechs	*6*
sieben	*7*
acht	*8*
neun	*9*
zehn	*10*
elf	*11*
zwölf	*12*
dreizehn	*13*
vierzehn	*14*
fünfzehn	*15*
sechzehn	*16*
siebzehn	*17*
achtzehn	*18*
neunzehn	*19*
zwanzig	*20*
Wann hast du Geburtstag?	*When is your birthday?*
Im Frühling.	*In the spring.*
Im Sommer.	*In the summer.*
Im Herbst.	*In the autumn.*
Im Winter.	*In the winter.*
Ich habe im Januar Geburtstag.	*My birthday is in January.*
Januar	*January*
Februar	*February*
März	*March*
April	*April*
Mai	*May*
Juni	*June*
Juli	*July*
August	*August*
September	*September*
Oktober	*October*
November	*November*
Dezember	*December*

Meine Klasse/ Schulsachen	***My class/Classroom objects***
Wer ist das?	*Who's that?*
Das ist der/ein Lehrer.	*That's the/a teacher (male).*
Das ist die/eine Lehrerin.	*That's the/a teacher (female).*
Das ist der/ein Schüler.	*That's the/a pupil (male).*
Das ist die/eine Schülerin.	*That's the/a pupil (female).*
Was ist das?	*What's that?*
Das ist …	*That's …*
der/ein Schreibtisch	*the/a desk*
der/ein Stuhl	*the/a chair*
die/eine Tafel	*the/a blackboard*
die/eine Tür	*the/a door*
die/eine Wand	*the/a wall*
das/ein Klassenzimmer	*the/a classroom*
das/ein Fenster	*the/a window*

Kannst du ...? Checklist

This is a checklist of the things you should aim to learn in German using Klasse! neu 1.
Use the **Check** boxes and the **Prove it!** column to keep track of what you have learned.

- ★ Tick the first box when you feel you are getting to grips with the learning objective, but sometimes need a prompt or time to think.
- ★ Tick the second box when you think you have fully mastered the learning objective and will be able to use it again in future.
- ★ Make notes following the prompts in the **Prove it!** column to help you show what you have learned. Your learning partner or parent can test you and initial the second box to confirm the progress you have made.

Learning objectives	**Check**		**Prove it!**
I can say 'Hello', 'Goodbye' and 'How are you?'	☐	☐	*Get partner to test you.*
I can introduce myself.	☐	☐	*Get partner to test you.*
I can ask someone his/her name.	☐	☐	*Get partner to test you.*
I can recite the German alphabet.	☐	☐	*Get partner to test you.*
I can count to 20.	☐	☐	*Get partner to test you.*
I can say and write the names of the months.	☐	☐	*Write them down without looking at your book.*
I can say and write the names of the seasons.	☐	☐	*Write them down without looking at your book.*
I can give my age.	☐	☐	*Get partner to test you.*
I can ask someone his/her age.	☐	☐	*Get partner to test you.*
I can say when my birthday is.	☐	☐	*Get partner to test you.*
I can ask when someone's birthday is.	☐	☐	*Get partner to test you.*
I can describe my classroom.	☐	☐	*Get partner to test you.*
I know it's important to learn the gender of a noun at the same time as the spelling and pronunciation.	☐	☐	*Explain why to a partner.*
I know the gender of some common nouns.	☐	☐	*Without looking at your book, write* der/die/das *for:* Lehrer, Schülerin, Klassenzimmer, Stuhl, Tafel.
I can form simple questions.	☐	☐	*Without looking at your book, write questions using:* wie, wann, wer, was.
I can recognize words for 'a' and 'the'.	☐	☐	*Get partner to test you.*
I can recognize the different sounds *ei* and *ie*.	☐	☐	*Read aloud:* ein, wie, drei, sieben, zwei, vier.
I can greet people appropriately.	☐	☐	*Get partner to test you.*
I can find six places on a map of Germany, Austria and Switzerland.	☐	☐	*Show a partner where to look.*

Haustiere

1 **Wie schreibt man diese Haustiere?**
What are the names of these animals in German?

a

b

c

d

e

f

g

h

i

j

ein Hund ein Hamster ein Fisch eine Schildkröte ein Pferd eine Maus
ein Meerschweinchen ein Wellensittich eine Katze ein Kaninchen

2 ***ein* oder *eine*? Füll die Lücken aus.**
ein *or* eine? *Fill in the blanks.*

a ______________ Pferd
b ______________ Maus
c ______________ Katze
d ______________ Hund
e ______________ Wellensittich
f ______________ Hamster
g ______________ Schildkröte
h ______________ Kaninchen

3 **Male die richtigen Farben.**
Colour in the squares.

Blau Schwarz Gelb Rot Braun Weiß Grau

Hast du ein Haustier?

1 Was passt zusammen?

Draw lines to match up the sentences and pictures.

1 Ich habe drei Fische, zwei Katzen und einen Hund.

2 Ich habe zwei Meerschweinchen, drei Mäuse und ein Pferd.

3 Ich habe einen Wellensittich, zwei Kaninchen und einen Hund.

4 Ich habe zwei Katzen, drei Hamster und eine Maus.

a

b

c

d

2 Was sagt Uli?

What does Uli say?

zwei Katzen	einen Wellensittich	vier Hunde	ein Pferd	einen Fisch	vier Fische
drei Meerschweinchen	drei Katzen	zwei Hunde	zwei Meerschweinchen	zwei Schildkröten	

____

____

____

____

Wie ist deine Familie?

1 **Worträtsel. Finde die Personen.**

Find the family members in the word square.

T	O	M	R	K	B	O	P	A	U
A	O	S	O	M	A	N	V	R	J
N	V	C	F	L	S	K	A	A	U
T	A	H	R	C	M	E	T	E	B
E	T	W	E	M	U	L	H	P	R
R	E	E	L	W	T	B	V	V	U
O	R	S	T	L	L	B	N	A	D
B	A	T	E	O	E	S	V	T	E
E	M	E	R	M	U	T	T	E	R
L	X	R	N	K	E	H	D	U	M

Bruder
Opa
Tante
Mutter
Onkel
Eltern
~~Oma~~
Schwester
Vater

2 **Füll die Lücken aus.**

Fill in the gaps to describe Karl's family.

Meine Mutter heißt Maria.

________________ heißt Ilse.

________________ heißt Jochen.

________________ heißt Sara.

________________ heißt Thomas.

________________ heißt Gisela.

________________ heißt Albrecht.

________________ heißt Stefan.

________________ heißt Anne.

________________ heißt David.

Wie bist du?

1 **Finde die Adjektive.**
Find the adjectives.

a NUJG ____________________
b NELILTETGNI ____________________
c NRETS ____________________
d ELKNI ____________________
e EDCRILHNUF ____________________
f ERFHC ____________________
g FELIßGI ____________________
h TAL ____________________
i TUAL ____________________
j AFLU ____________________
k ELSEI ____________________
l RGOß ____________________
m SRLTCIHPO ____________________
n SKUIIASLHCM ____________________

2 **Du bist dran! Beschreib drei Personen in deiner Familie.**
Describe three people in your family.

groß	klein	sportlich	jung	alt	musikalisch	laut
leise	faul	intelligent	frech	fleißig	ernst	freundlich

Vater	sehr
Mutter	ziemlich
Bruder	nicht
Schwester	gar nicht
Onkel	
Tante	
Opa	
Oma	

Beispiel: *Mein Bruder ist sehr freundlich, aber gar nicht alt. Er ist nicht sportlich, aber sehr fleißig. Er ist sehr laut und ziemlich klein.*

1 ____

____

____

2 ____

____

____

3 ____

____

____

Brieffreunde

1 **Welche Fragen und Antworten passen zusammen?**
Draw lines to match up the questions and answers.

1 Wie heißt du?
2 Wie alt bist du?
3 Wann hast du Geburtstag?
4 Wie heißt dein Vater?
5 Wie ist deine Mutter?
6 Wie alt ist deine Schwester?
7 Wie alt ist dein Bruder?
8 Hast du Haustiere?

a Er heißt Alf.
b Im Winter.
c Sie ist sportlich und intelligent.
d Er ist 18 Jahre alt.
e Sie ist 14 Jahre alt.
f Ich bin 12 Jahre alt.
g Ja, ich habe ein Kaninchen.
h Ich heiße Monika.

2 **Wähle die richtige Antwort.**
Choose the correct answer.

Ich heiße/habe Max und ich bin/bist 13 Jahre alt. Ich habe/hast im April Geburtstag. Ich habe eine/ein Schwester. Er/sie heißt Tanja und sie bin/ist 12 Jahre alt. Sie bist/ist intelligent und auch sehr sportlich. Ich habe einen/eine Katze. Sie ist alt und sehr freundlich.

3 **Beschreib zwei Personen mit den folgenden Vokabeln.**
Write sentences to describe two people using some of the following words.

sehr	ziemlich
nicht	auch
und	aber

Beispiel: *Mein Bruder heißt Karl. Er ist ziemlich intelligent, aber nicht sehr freundlich.*

Grammatik 1

Flashback

Maskulinum	Femininum	Neutrum	
ein	eine	ein	*a*
er	sie	es	*it*

1 **Füll die Lücken mit *er, sie* oder *es* aus.**
***Fill in the gaps with* er, sie *or* es.**

a Das ist ein Hund. ___Er___ ist braun.

b Das ist eine Schildkröte. __________ ist grün.

c Das ist ein Pferd. __________ ist schwarz.

d Das ist eine Katze. __________ ist braun und weiß.

e Das ist ein Meerschweinchen. __________ ist klein.

f Das ist ein Fisch. __________ ist rot und blau.

2 **Finde die passenden Bilder.**
Match the sentences to the correct picture.

Flashback

To make most English nouns plural, you add an -s. German nouns form their plurals in different ways:

eine Katze	→	zwei Katze**n**
ein Fisch	→	zwei Fisch**e**
eine Maus	→	zwei M**ä**us**e**
ein Meerschweinchen	→	zwei Meerschweinchen

Beispiel: *Ich habe zwei Pferde.* [a]

1 Ich habe eine Maus. [ ]

2 Ich habe zwei Katzen. [ ]

3 Ich habe drei Hunde. [ ]

4 Ich habe eine Katze. [ ]

5 Ich habe zwei Meerschweinchen. [ ]

6 Ich habe einen Fisch. [ ]

7 Ich habe drei Fische. [ ]

8 Ich habe vier Mäuse. [ ]

a

b

c

d

e

f

g

h

i

Grammatik 2

1 **Wähle die richtige Antwort.**
Underline the correct answer.

a Meine Schwester habe/hat im Juli Geburtstag.
b Mein Hund heiße/heißt Max.
c Wann hast/hat du Geburtstag?
d Mein Bruder bist/ist 14 Jahre alt.
e Wie alt bist/ist du?
f Ich habe/hat im Juni Geburtstag.
g Ich bin/bist 12 Jahre alt.

Flashback

Remember the different endings and verb forms:

ich	bin	habe	heiße
du	bist	hast	heißt
er/sie/es	ist	hat	heißt

2a **Schreib die Sätze richtig auf.**
Write the sentences in the correct order.

1 Meerschweinchen habe ich ein

____

2 klein es und ist weiß

____

3 sehr mein Großvater ist alt

____

4 Schwester Mai im hat Geburtstag meine

____

5 Jahre 44 alt ist Vater mein

____

6 freundlich Mutter ist und leise meine

____

2b **Schreib die Antworten auf Englisch auf.**
Now translate your answers into English.

1 ______________________________
2 ______________________________
3 ______________________________
4 ______________________________
5 ______________________________
6 ______________________________

Haustiere	***Pets***
Das ist ...	*That is ...*
ein Hund	*a dog*
ene Katze	*a cat*
ein Fisch	*a fish*
ein Wellensittich	*a budgie*
eine Schildkröte	*a tortoise*
ein Pferd	*a horse*
ein Hamster	*a hamster*
ein Meerschweinchen	*a guinea pig*
ein Kaninchen	*a rabbit*
eine Maus	*a mouse*
Er/sie/es ist ...	*It is ...*
blau	*blue*
braun	*brown*
rot	*red*
grün	*green*
gelb	*yellow*
schwarz	*black*
weiß	*white*
orange	*orange*
grau	*grey*

Hast du ein Haustier?	***Have you got a pet?***
Ich habe ...	*I have ...*
einen Hund	*a dog*
eine Katze	*a cat*
ein Meerschweinchen	*a guinea pig*
zwei Pferde	*two horses*
zwei Schildkröten	*two tortoises*
zwei Mäuse	*two mice*
Ich habe keine Haustiere.	*I don't have any pets.*

Wie ist deine Familie?	***What's your family like?***
Hast du Geschwister?	*Do you have brothers and sisters?*
Ich habe ...	*I have ...*
einen Bruder/eine Schwester	*a brother/a sister*
einen Halbbruder/eine Halbschwester	*a half-brother/a half-sister*
einen Stiefbruder/eine Stiefschwester	*a stepbrother/a stepsister*
zwei Brüder/zwei Schwestern	*two brothers/ two sisters*
Ich habe keine Geschwister.	*I have no brothers and sisters.*
Ich bin Einzelkind.	*I am an only child.*
Das ist ...	*That is ...*
mein Bruder/mein Halbbruder	*my brother/my half-brother*
meine Schwester/meine Halbschwester	*my sister/my half-sister*
mein Vater/mein Stiefvater	*my father/my stepfather*
meine Mutter/meine Stiefmutter	*my mother/my stepmother*
mein Onkel	*my uncle*
meine Tante	*my aunt*
mein Großvater	*my grandfather*
meine Großmutter	*my grandmother*
mein Cousin	*my cousin (m.)*
meine Cousine	*my cousin (f.)*
Wie heißt dein Vater/deine Mutter?	*What is your father/mother called?*

Wie bist du?	***What are you like?***
musikalisch	*musical*
fleißig	*hard-working*
jung	*young*
freundlich	*friendly*
frech	*cheeky*
alt	*old*
ernst	*serious*
groß	*tall*
faul	*lazy*
leise	*quiet*
intelligent	*intelligent*
sportlich	*sporty*
klein	*small*
laut	*loud*
sehr	*very*
ziemlich	*quite*
nicht	*not*
gar nicht	*not at all*
Wie ist dein Bruder/deine Schwester?	*What is your brother/your sister like?*

Kannst du ...? Checklist

This is a checklist of the things you should aim to learn in German using Klasse! neu 1.
Use the **Check** boxes and the **Prove it!** column to keep track of what you have learned.

- Tick the first box when you feel you are getting to grips with the learning objective, but sometimes need a prompt or time to think.
- Tick the second box when you think you have fully mastered the learning objective and will be able to use it again in future.
- Make notes following the prompts in the **Prove it!** column to help you show what you have learned. Your learning partner or parent can test you and initial the second box to confirm the progress you have made.

Learning objectives	Check		Prove it!
I can say whether I have pets.	☐	☐	*Get partner to test you.*
I can ask someone whether he/she has any pets.	☐	☐	*Get partner to test you.*
I can say and write the names of eight pets.	☐	☐	*Write them down and say aloud to a partner.*
I can say what colour pets are.	☐	☐	*Get partner to test you.*
I can say and write the names of family members.	☐	☐	*Write them down and say aloud to a partner.*
I can describe myself and members of my family.	☐	☐	*Get partner to test you.*
I can ask someone if he/she has any brothers and sisters.	☐	☐	*Get partner to test you.*
I can say if I have any brothers and sisters.	☐	☐	*Get partner to test you.*
I can ask what somebody's name is.	☐	☐	*Get partner to test you.*
I can give two different words for 'my' and explain why there are two.	☐	☐	*Get partner to test you.*
I can use *einen/eine/ein* and *keinen/keine/kein* correctly after *ich habe ...*	☐	☐	*Get partner to test you.*
I can write a longer description.	☐	☐	*Get partner to test you.*
I know some high-frequency words and understand their importance.	☐	☐	*Choose which three of the following are high-frequency, give their meaning and use them in a sentence:* sehr, alt, und, Katze, aber, Bruder.

Meine Schulsachen

1 Was hast du? Finde die passenden Bilder.

Find the correct words for the pictures.

a

b
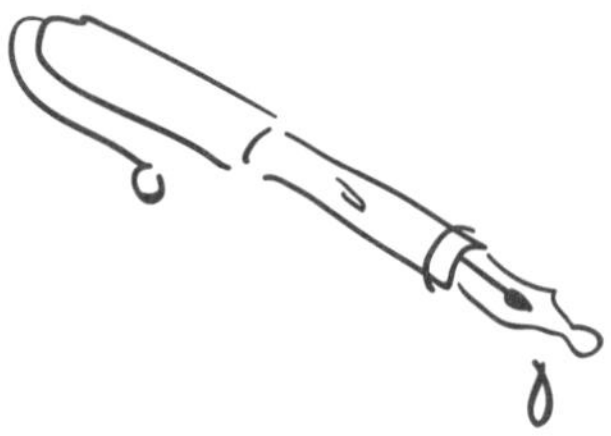

c
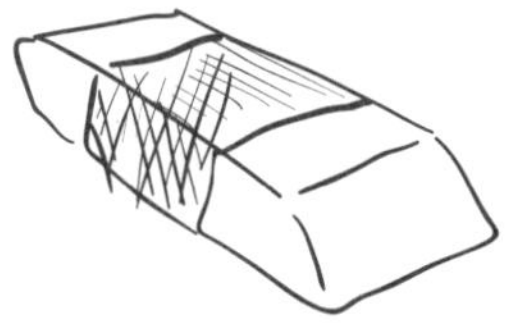

d
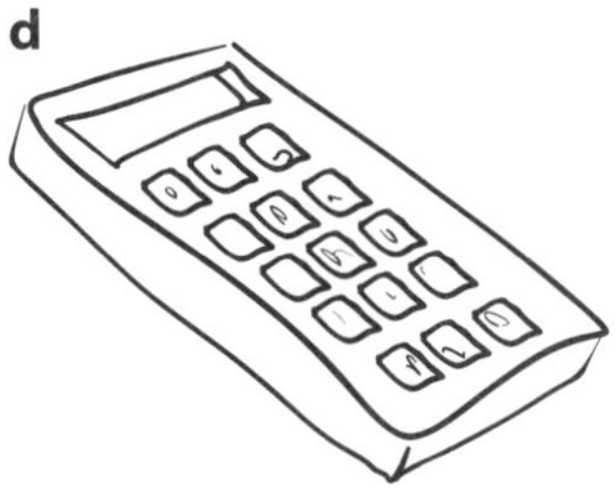

e
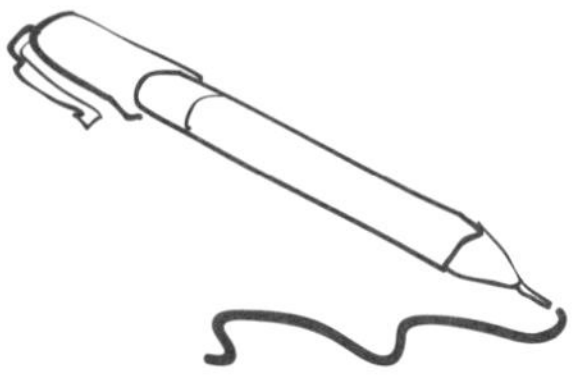

f

g
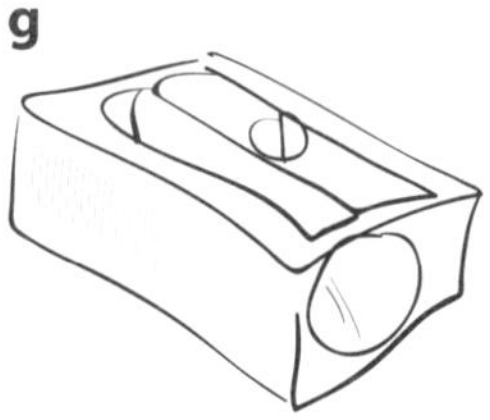

h

Ich habe …

1 einen Rechner [d]

2 einen Filzstift [ ]

3 ein Buch [ ]

4 einen Anspitzer [ ]

5 ein Heft [ ]

6 einen Füller [ ]

7 eine Tasche [ ]

8 einen Radiergummi [ ]

2 Finde die passenden Wörter.

Underline the correct article for each sentence.

a Ich habe eine/einen Kuli.

b Hast du ein/eine Heft?

c Ich habe ein/eine Tasche.

d Ich habe einen/eine Bleistift.

e Hast du ein/einen Lineal?

f Ich habe einen/ein Buch.

3 Was hat Maxi-Monster?

Complete the sentence.

Ich habe __________ __________, __________

__________ und __________ __________.

Schulfächer

1 **Finde die Schulfächer und schreib sie auf Deutsch und auf Englisch auf.**
Write down the jumbled-up school subjects in German and in English.

a	KUN ERD DE	Erdkunde	geography
b	GIE LO BIO		
c	LISCH ENG		
d	TIK IN MA FOR		
e	LI RE GION		
f	ZÖ SISCH FRAN		

2 **„Wie ist …?“ Schreib Sätze.**
Follow the lines and write sentences.

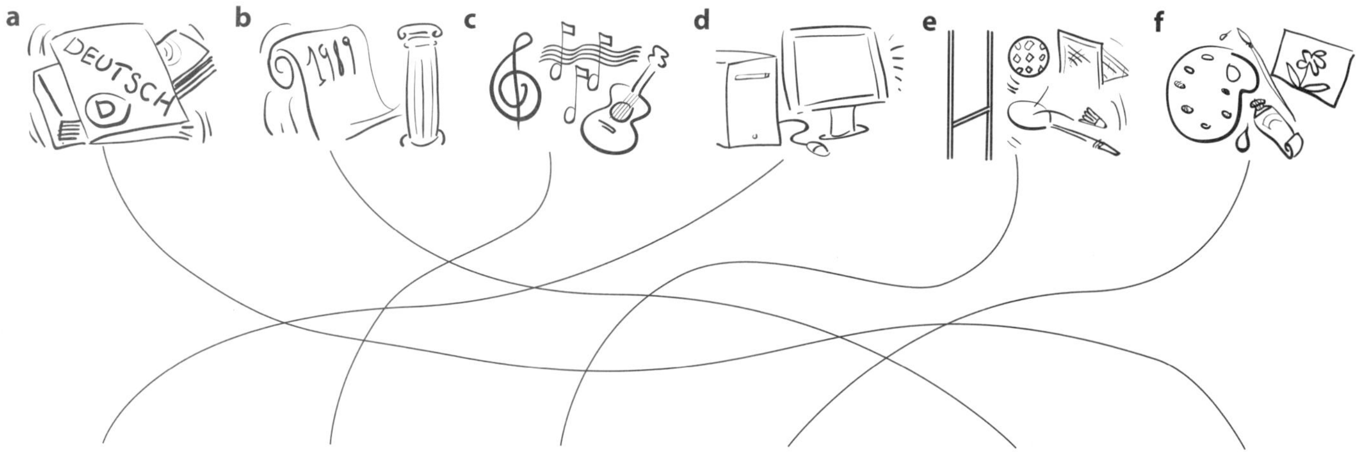

schwer interessant super doof langweilig prima

Beispiel:

a Deutsch ist prima!

b __________

c __________

d __________

e __________

f __________

Wie spät ist es?

1 Finde die richtige Reihenfolge.

Write down the sentences correctly.

a Viertel | Es | drei | ist | vor | . — Es ist Viertel vor drei.

b ist | spät | es | Wie | ? — ____________________

c neun | Es | Uhr | ist | . — ____________________

d drei | ist | Es | halb | . — ____________________

2 Finde die passenden Sätze.

Match the pictures with the sentences.

a [5] b [ ] c [ ] d [ ] e [ ] f [ ]

1 Es ist Viertel nach acht.
2 Es ist Viertel vor eins.
3 Es ist zehn Uhr.
4 Es ist halb acht.
5 Es ist Viertel vor elf.
6 Es ist halb eins.

3a Zeichne die richtigen Uhrzeiten auf.

Draw the correct time on the clocks.

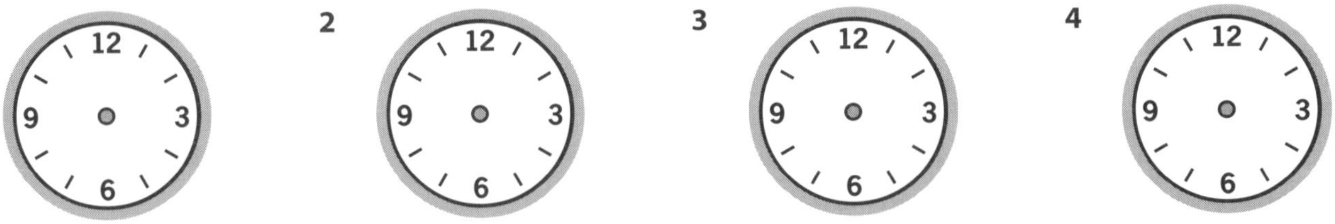

1 Es ist Viertel nach elf.
2 Es ist Mittag.
3 Es ist halb vier.
4 Es ist sieben Uhr.

3b Schreib die richtigen Uhrzeiten auf.

Write the correct time.

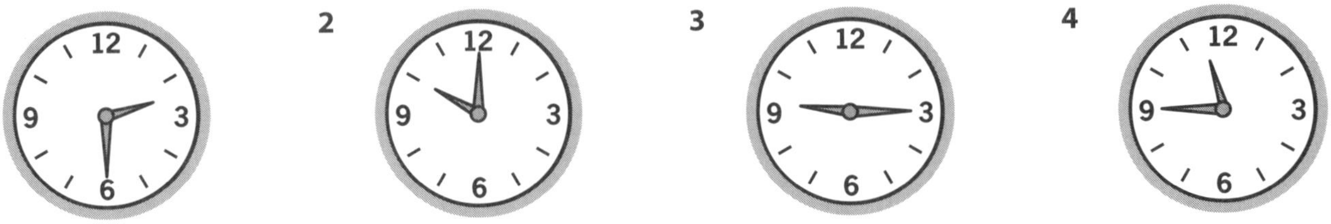

1 Es ist ____________________

2 ____________________

3 ____________________

4 ____________________

Mein Schultag

1a **Füll die Lücken aus.**
Fill in the gaps.

1 Dienstag

2 D_ _ne_s_ag

3 Fr_ _ta_

4 M_ _tw_ch

5 Mo_ _ _g

6 Sa_st_ _

7 S_ _nt_ _

1b **Schreib die richtige Reihenfolge auf.**
Write the days in the correct order.

1c **Wie heißt das auf Englisch?**
Write the English.

Montag	Monday

2 **Schreib die Sätze richtig auf.**
Write the sentences in the correct order.

a Am Montag: Mathe — Am Montag habe ich Mathe.

b Am Dienstag: Deutsch ____________

c Am Mittwoch: Musik ____________

d Am Donnerstag: Informatik ____________

e Am Freitag: Französisch ____________

f Am Samstag: Sport ____________

g Am Sonntag: frei! ____________

Verben im Präsens

1 **Finde die passenden Wörter auf Englisch.**
Find the correct pronouns in English.

a ich	**1** *you (to an adult)*
b du	**2** *I*
c er	**3** *we*
d sie	**4** *they*
e wir	**5** *he*
f ihr	**6** *you (to a friend)*
g Sie	**7** *she*
h sie	**8** *you (to several friends)*

Flashback

schreiben

ich	schreibe
du	schreibst
er/sie	schreibt
wir	schreiben
ihr	schreibt
sie/Sie	schreiben

2 **Unterstreiche die passenden Wörter.**
Underline the correct verb forms.

a Ich finde/finden Deutsch prima.

b Er macht/machst Pause.

c Wie heiße/heißt du?

d Ihr hören/hört gut zu.

e Sie schreibst/schreiben eine E-Mail.

f Wie findest/finde du Mathe?

g Wir machen/macht Hausaufgaben.

3 **Füll die Lücken aus.**
Fill in the gaps.

a Wie find__________ du Sport?

b Sie heiß__________ Melanie.

c Er mach__________ seine Hausaufgaben.

d Sie heiß__________ Tom and Tina.

e Wir schreib__________ einen Dialog.

> **Flashback**
>
> **sie** = *she + they* **Sie** = *you (polite)*

1 Schreib *she, they* oder *you* für die Sätze.
Write she, they *or* you *under the sentences.*

a

Haben Sie ein Heft?

you

b

Sie ist vierzehn Jahre alt.

____

c

Sie sind sehr klein!

____

d

Wann haben Sie Kunst?

____

e

Sie haben einen Hund.

____

f

Sie ist sehr sportlich!

____

> **Flashback**
>
> Ich habe am Freitag Kunst. → Am Freitag habe ich Kunst.

2 Schreib Sätze.
Complete the sentences.
Beispiel:

a Am Montag habe ich Sport.

b Am Dienstag ______________________.

c Am Mittwoch ______________________.

d Am Donnerstag ______________________.

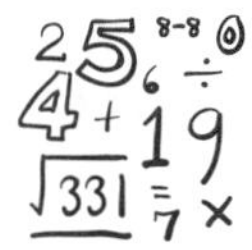

e Am Freitag ______________________.

f Am Samstag ______________________.

Grammatik 2

Flashback

haben ***to have***
ich habe
du hast
er/sie/es hat
wir haben
ihr habt
sie/Sie haben

1 **Füll die Sätze mit *haben* aus.**
***Fill in the correct form of the verb* haben.**

a Wir ____________ Englisch.

b Susi ____________ kein Heft.

c ____________ Sie ein Lineal, Frau May?

d Ich ____________ am Montag Sport.

e ____________ ihr ein Buch?

f Wann ____________ du Naturwissenschaften?

Flashback

sein ***to be***
ich bin
du bist
er/sie/es ist
wir sind
ihr seid
sie/Sie sind

2 **Füll die Sätze mit *sein* aus.**
***Fill in the correct form of the verb* sein.**

a Ich ____________ dreizehn Jahre alt.

b Mathe ____________ mein Lieblingsfach.

c Das ____________ meine Eltern.

d ____________ du vierzehn Jahre alt?

e Ihr ____________ musikalisch.

f Wir ____________ sportlich.

3 ***Haben* oder *sein*? Unterstreiche die richtige Antwort.**
Haben *or* sein? *Underline the correct verb.*

a Wir haben/sind um neun Uhr Deutsch.

b Es ist/hat halb zwölf.

c Bist/Hast du ein Lineal?

d Ich bin/habe keinen Anspitzer.

e Ihr habt/seid fünfzehn Jahre alt.

f Wann haben/sind sie Mathe?

Meine Schulsachen	***My classroom objects***
Hast du …?	*Do you have …? (informal)*
Haben Sie …?	*Do you have …? (formal)*
einen Bleistift	*a pencil*
einen Filzstift	*a felt-tip pen*
einen Füller	*a fountain pen*
einen Kuli	*a ballpoint pen*
einen Rechner	*a calculator*
einen Radiergummi	*a rubber*
einen Anspitzer	*a pencil sharpener*
eine Tasche	*a bag*
ein Buch	*a book*
ein Heft	*an exercise book*
ein Lineal	*a ruler*
Ja, ich habe …	*Yes, I have …*
Hier, bitte.	*Here you are.*
Nein, leider nicht.	*No, sorry.*
Ich habe keinen Kuli.	*I don't have a pen.*
Ich habe keine Tasche.	*I don't have a bag.*
Ich habe kein Buch.	*I don't have a book.*

Schulfächer	***School subjects***
Deutsch	*German*
Englisch	*English*
Erdkunde	*Geography*
Französisch	*French*
Geschichte	*History*
Informatik	*IT*
Kunst	*Art*
Mathe	*Maths*
Musik	*Music*
Naturwissenschaften (Biologie, Chemie, Physik)	*Science (Biology, Chemistry, Physics)*
Religion	*Religious Studies*
Sport	*PE*
Was ist dein Lieblingsfach?	*What's your favourite subject?*
Mein Lieblingsfach ist Sport.	*My favourite subject is PE.*
Wie findest du Sport?	*What do you think of PE?*
Sport ist …	*PE is …*
prima/super	*excellent/great*
fantastisch/interessant	*fantastic/interesting*
furchtbar/langweilig	*awful/boring*
doof	*stupid*

Wie spät ist es?	***What time is it?***
Wie spät ist es?	*What time is it?*
Es ist …	*It is …*
zwei Uhr	*two o'clock*
halb zwei	*half past one*
Viertel vor zwei	*quarter to two*
Viertel nach zwei	*quarter past two*
Mittag	*noon*
Mitternacht	*midnight*

Mein Schultag	***My school day***
Wann hast du …?	*When do you have …?*
Wann haben wir …?	*When do we have …?*
Um neun Uhr.	*At nine o'clock.*
Was hast du am …?	*What do you have on …?*
Am … habe ich …	*On … I have …*
Montag	*Monday*
Dienstag	*Tuesday*
Mittwoch	*Wednesday*
Donnerstag	*Thursday*
Freitag	*Friday*
Samstag	*Saturday*
Sonntag	*Sunday*
Am Samstag habe ich frei!	*On Saturdays, I'm free!*
Am Sonntag habe ich keine Schule!	*On Sundays, I don't have school!*

Kannst du ...? Checklist

This is a checklist of the things you should aim to learn in German using Klasse! neu 1.
Use the **Check** boxes and the **Prove it!** column to keep track of what you have learned.

★ Tick the first box when you feel you are getting to grips with the learning objective, but sometimes need a prompt or time to think.

★ Tick the second box when you think you have fully mastered the learning objective and will be able to use it again in future.

★ Make notes following the prompts in the **Prove it!** column to help you show what you have learned. Your learning partner or parent can test you and initial the second box to confirm the progress you have made.

Learning objectives	**Check**		**Prove it!**
I can ask someone what classroom objects he/she has.	☐	☐	*Get partner to test you.*
I can say what classroom objects I have/don't have.	☐	☐	*Get partner to test you.*
I can ask for classroom objects from my partner/teacher.	☐	☐	*Get partner/teacher to test you.*
I can ask someone which school subjects he/she likes.	☐	☐	*Get partner to test you.*
I can say which subjects I like and dislike.	☐	☐	*Get partner to test you.*
I can give opinions.	☐	☐	*Get partner to test you.*
I can ask and say the time.	☐	☐	*Get partner to test you.*
I can ask when someone has different subjects.	☐	☐	*Get partner to test you.*
I can say when I have different subjects.	☐	☐	*Get partner to test you.*
I can say the days of the week.	☐	☐	*Get partner to test you.*
I can read a German timetable.	☐	☐	*Check the timetable on page 43 of the Students' Book again.*
I can use *du, ihr* or *Sie* correctly when I say 'you' to different people.	☐	☐	*Get partner to test you.*
I know the present tense of *sein.*	☐	☐	*Get partner to test you.*
I know the present tense of *haben.*	☐	☐	*Get partner to test you.*
I know the present tense of some weak/regular verbs.	☐	☐	*How do you say: I find, he finds, Ellen and Max find? Check your answers with a partner.*
I can write a sentence in German where the verb always comes second.	☐	☐	*Get partner to test you.*
I can use different strategies to learn new words.	☐	☐	*Tell a partner what you might do to learn new words.*
I know some of the differences between German and British schools.	☐	☐	*Tell a partner three differences.*

4.1 Meine Adresse

1 **Was passt zusammen?**
Match up the numbers and words.

a	b	c	d	e	f	g	h
37	98	63	71	82	54	49	26
☐	☐	☐	☐	☐	☐	☐	☐

1 achtundneunzig
2 einundsiebzig
3 vierundfünfzig
4 siebenunddreißig
5 sechsundzwanzig
6 zweiundachtzig
7 dreiundsechzig
8 neunundvierzig

2 **Wo wohnt Familie Maus?**
Where does the Maus family live? Follow the lines and write the numbers.

Beispiel: Milli – Nummer neununddreißig.

____

3 **Schreib Sätze.**
Write sentences to answer these questions.

Wo wohnst du? ____________________

Wie ist deine Adresse? ____________________

Mein Haus

1 **Was ist das? Schreib die passenden Wörter auf.**
What is it? Fill in the correct words.

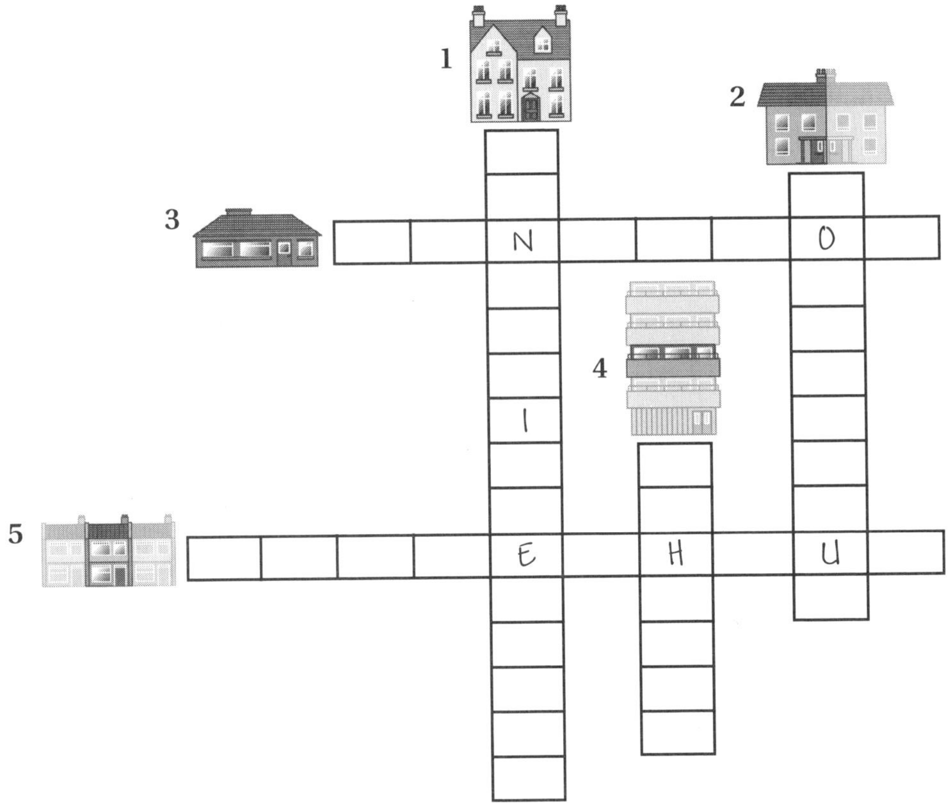

2 **Was passt zusammen?**
Draw lines to match up the sentence halves.

1  Tanja wohnt — **a** in der Stadt.

2  Olaf wohnt — **b** am Stadtrand.

3  Wiebke wohnt — **c** in einem Dorf.

4  Johannes wohnt — **d** in einer Wohnsiedlung.

5  Ilka wohnt — **e** auf dem Land.

Und das ist die Küche …

1 **Finde die passenden Zimmer.**
Match the room with the correct word in the box.

a die Küche **b** die Dusche **c** der Balkon **d** das Badezimmer **e** das Schlafzimmer **f** das Esszimmer **g** das Wohnzimmer

2 **Beschreib das Haus. Füll die Lücken aus.**
Fill in the gaps to describe the house.

Beispiel: *Die Küche ist im Erdgeschoss. Sie ist groß und modern.*

a Die Schlafzimmer sind im e_______________ Stock. Sie sind g_______________ und s_______________.

b Die Dusche ist im z_______________ Stock. Sie ist k_______________ und m_______________.

c Das Esszimmer ist im E_______________. Es ist k_______________ und h_______________.

d Das Wohnzimmer ist im E_______________. Es ist h_______________ und u_______________.

e Das Badezimmer ist im e_______________ S_______________. Es ist g_______________, aber a_______________.

f Der Balkon ist im z_______________ S_______________. Er ist k_______________, aber s_______________.

Mein Zimmer

1 Füll die Lücken aus.

Fill in the gaps.

a

ein Co__p__t__r

b
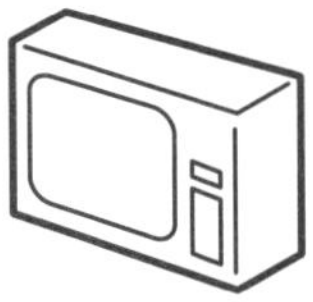
ein __er__sehe__

c

ein K__eid__rs__hr__nk

d
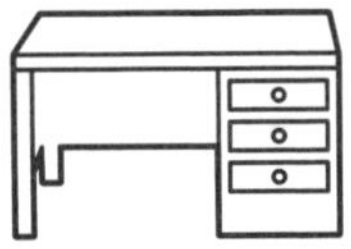
ein Sc__rei__t__s__h

e

eine L__mp__

f

ein S__ __hl

g

ein B__t__

h
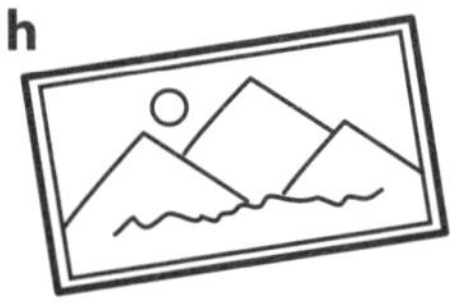
ein Pos__e__

i

eine St__r__o__n__ag__

j

ein Re__a__

k
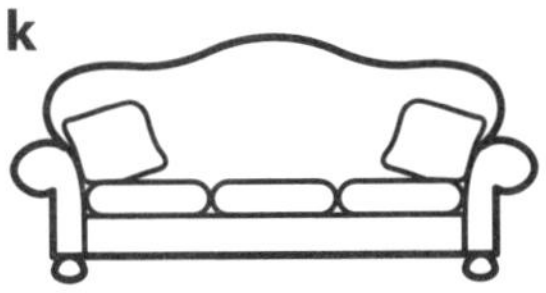
ein __o__a

2 Ist das richtig (R) oder falsch (F)?

True or false?

a Der Fernseher ist auf dem Tisch. ☐

b Die Stereoanlage ist unter dem Regal. ☐
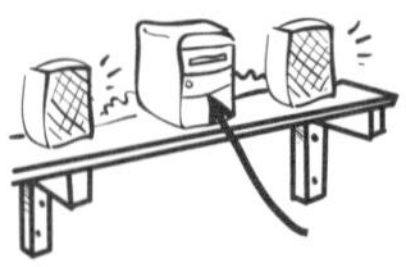

c Die Kleidung ist unter dem Bett. ☐
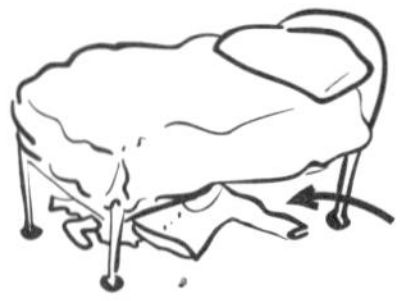

d Der Schreibtisch ist hinter dem Sofa. ☐

e Der Kleiderschrank ist zwischen dem Sofa und dem Bett. ☐

f Der Stuhl ist hinter dem Schreibtisch. ☐

Grammatik 1

1 **Füll die Lücken aus: *einem* oder *einer*?**
***Fill in the gaps:* einem *or* einer?**

> **Flashback**
>
> Ich wohne in **einem** Reihenhaus.
> Ich wohne in **einer** Wohnung.

a Ich wohne in ______________ Bungalow.

b Ich wohne in ______________ Wohnung.

c Ich wohne in ______________ Doppelhaus.

d Ich wohne in ______________ Reihenhaus.

2 **Füll die Lücken aus.**
Fill in the gaps.

1 Ich wohne in ________________________ Dorf.

2 Ich wohne ________________________ Stadtrand.

3 Ich wohne auf ________________________ Land.

4 Ich wohne in ________________________ Stadt.

5 Ich wohne in ________________________ Wohnsiedlung.

am
dem
der
einem
einer

3 **Was gibt es in deinem Zimmer?**
What is there in your room?

a **b** **c** **d** **e** **f** **g** **h**

In meinem Zimmer gibt es …

Beispiel:

a ein Bett ________________________ **e** ________________________

b ________________________ **f** ________________________

c ________________________ **g** ________________________

d ________________________ **h** ________________________

Grammatik 2

Flashback

auf **dem** Tisch **(masc.)** neben **der** Lampe **(fem.)** unter **dem** Bett **(neut.)**

1 **Wo sind die Möbelstücke? Wähle die richtige Antwort.**
Where are the items of furniture? Choose the correct answer.

- **a** Das Bett ist neben/unter dem Kleiderschrank.
- **b** Der Kleiderschrank ist zwischen/auf dem Bett und dem Regal.
- **c** Der Stuhl ist unter/auf dem Tisch.
- **d** Die Lampe ist hinter/unter dem Fernseher.
- **e** Die Stereoanlage ist auf/vor dem Regal.
- **f** Die Kleidung ist vor/unter dem Bett.
- **g** Der Fernseher ist hinter/vor der Lampe.
- **h** Das Regal ist neben/unter dem Bett.

2 **Beantworte die Fragen auf Deutsch.**
Answer the questions in German for yourself.

a Wo wohnst du?

Ich wohne in ______________________________

b Wie ist deine Adresse?

Meine Adresse ist ______________________________

c Was gibt es in deinem Haus?

In meinem Haus gibt es ______________________________

____

d Wie ist dein Zimmer?

Mein Zimmer ist ______________________________

e Was gibt es in deinem Zimmer?

In meinem Zimmer gibt es ______________________________

____

f Wo sind die Möbelstücke?

Das Bett ist ______________________________

____

Meine Adresse	***My address***
Wo wohnst du?	*Where do you live?*
Wie ist deine Adresse?	*What is your address?*
Meine Adresse ist ...	*My address is ...*
Meine Hausnummer ist ...	*My house number is ...*
zwanzig	*twenty*
dreißig	*thirty*
vierzig	*forty*
fünfzig	*fifty*
sechzig	*sixty*
siebzig	*seventy*
achtzig	*eighty*
neunzig	*ninety*
hundert	*one hundred*

Mein Haus	***My house***
Ich wohne ...	*I live ...*
in einem Bungalow	*in a bungalow*
in einem Einfamilienhaus	*in a detached house*
in einem Doppelhaus	*in a semi-detached house*
in einem Reihenhaus	*in a terraced house*
in einer Wohnung	*in a flat*
am Stadtrand	*on the edge of town*
in einem Dorf	*in a village*
in der Stadt	*in the town*
in einer Wohnsiedlung	*in a residential area*
auf dem Land	*in the country*

Und das ist die Küche ...	***And this is the kitchen ...***
das Badezimmer	*the bathroom*
die Dusche	*the shower*
das Esszimmer	*the dining-room*
die Garage	*the garage*
der Garten	*the garden*
der Keller	*the cellar*
die Küche	*the kitchen*
das Schlafzimmer	*the bedroom*
das Wohnzimmer	*the living-room*
im Erdgeschoss	*on the ground floor*
im ersten Stock	*on the first floor*
im zweiten Stock	*on the second floor*
In meinem Haus gibt es ein Esszimmer, einen Garten und eine Garage.	*In my house there is a dining-room, a garden and a garage.*

Mein Zimmer	***My room***
das Bett	*the bed*
der Computer	*the computer*
der Fernseher	*the television*
der Kleiderschrank	*the wardrobe*
die Lampe	*the lamp*
das Poster	*the poster*
das Regal	*the shelf*
der Schreibtisch	*the desk*
das Sofa	*the sofa*
die Stereoanlage	*the stereo*
der Stuhl	*the chair*
die Kleidung	*the clothes*
auf	*on*
hinter	*behind*
in	*in*
neben	*next to*
über	*above*
unter	*under*
vor	*in front of*
zwischen	*between*
In meinem Zimmer gibt es eine Stereoanlage.	*In my room there is a stereo.*
Die Stereoanlage ist auf dem Regal.	*The stereo is on the shelf.*
groß	*big*
modern	*modern*
klein	*small*
alt	*old*
unordentlich	*untidy*
schön	*beautiful/pretty*
hässlich	*ugly*

Kannst du …? Checklist

This is a checklist of the things you should aim to learn in German using Klasse! neu 1.
Use the **Check** boxes and the **Prove it!** column to keep track of what you have learned.

- Tick the first box when you feel you are getting to grips with the learning objective, but sometimes need a prompt or time to think.
- Tick the second box when you think you have fully mastered the learning objective and will be able to use it again in future.
- Make notes following the prompts in the **Prove it!** column to help you show what you have learned. Your learning partner or parent can test you and initial the second box to confirm the progress you have made.

Learning objectives	Check		Prove it!
I can count up to 100.	☐	☐	*Get partner to test you.*
I can give my address and house number.	☐	☐	*Get partner to test you.*
I can ask someone for his/her address.	☐	☐	*Get partner to test you.*
I can describe where I live.	☐	☐	*Get partner to test you.*
I can ask someone about where he/she lives.	☐	☐	*Get partner to test you.*
I can describe my house or flat.	☐	☐	*Get partner to test you.*
I can say and write five different types of home.	☐	☐	*Write them down without looking at the book.*
I can say and write the names of different rooms in my home.	☐	☐	*Write them down without looking at the book.*
I can say where the different rooms are.	☐	☐	*Get partner to test you.*
I can say what is in my room.	☐	☐	*Get partner to test you.*
I can say where things are in my room.	☐	☐	*Get partner to test you.*
I can improve my reading skills by using a checklist.	☐	☐	*Explain to a partner.*
I can use a checklist to improve my written work.	☐	☐	*List three strategies that you would use here.*
I can work out some new words when reading.	☐	☐	*Explain to a partner three ways to do this.*
I know how to check my work for spellings and the gender of nouns.	☐	☐	*Explain to a partner three ways to do this.*
I can use the correct form of *ein/eine/ein* after *es gibt.*	☐	☐	*Explain the rule to a partner.*
I can use the correct form of *ein/eine/ein* after prepositions.	☐	☐	*Explain the rule to a partner.*

Etwas zum Essen

1 **Was ist alles in Cedis Kühlschrank? Schreib die Wörter auf.**
Write in the names of the items of food and drink in the fridge.

Beispiel:

a Wurst

b ____________

c ____________

d ____________

e ____________

f ____________

g ____________

h ____________

i ____________

j ____________

k ____________

l ____________

m ____________

n ____________

o ____________

Jogurt Brötchen ein Apfel Orangensaft
Kartoffeln Milch eine Banane Fisch Cola Brot
Nudeln Salat Wurst Käse

2 **Lies den Speiseplan und füll die Lücken aus.**
Fill in the gaps in the meal planner.

Montag

B__o__ mit Kä__ __, ein Ap__ __l

Dienstag

W__r__ __ mit Ka__t__f__el__, ein J__g__r__

Mittwoch

F__ __ __h mit S__l__ t, M__l__h

Donnerstag

B__ö__c__e__ mit E__, O__a__g__n__a__t

Freitag

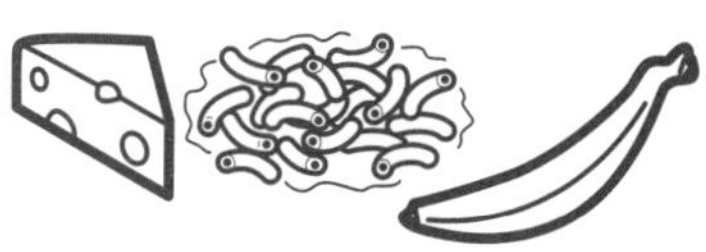

N__d__l__ mit K__s__, eine B__n__n__

1 Finde 12 Frühstück-Wörter.

Find 12 items of breakfast food and drink in the word search.

V	K	A	F	F	E	E	R	M	Ü	S	L	I
P	R	M	A	R	M	E	L	A	D	E	W	S
R	T	C	O	R	N	F	L	A	K	E	S	G
Y	X	H	O	N	I	G	K	J	T	E	E	H
F	D	W	B	R	Ö	T	C	H	E	N	P	M
C	B	U	T	T	E	R	Z	M	I	L	C	H
C	G	O	R	A	N	G	E	N	S	A	F	T
W	F	K	A	K	A	O	H	B	R	O	T	Z

2 Was isst du zum Mittagessen? Schreib die Sätze richtig auf.

Write down the sentences correctly.

a [esse] [Wurst] [Mittagessen] [Zum] [ich] [.] Zum Mittagessen esse ich Wurst.

b [ich] [Mittagessen] [esse] [Nudeln] [Zum] [.] ______

c [Salat] [Zum] [ich] [Mittagessen] [esse] [.] ______

d [Zum] [Pommes] [frites] [esse] [ich] [Mittagessen] [.] ______

e [Mittagessen] [ich] [Zum] [esse] [Fisch] [.] ______

f [esse] [ich] [Mittagessen] [Brot] [Zum] [.] ______

5.3 Ich esse kein Fleisch!

Guten Appetit!

1 **Finde die passsenden Bilder für die Sätze.**
Draw lines to match the sentences to the pictures.

a

b

c

d

1 Ich esse nicht gern Obst!

2 Ich trinke keine Cola.

3 Ich esse gern Wurst!

4 Ich esse keine Pommes frites.

2 **Was isst und trinkt Tom nicht? Füll die Lücken aus.**
What does Tom not eat and drink? Complete the speech bubbles for him.

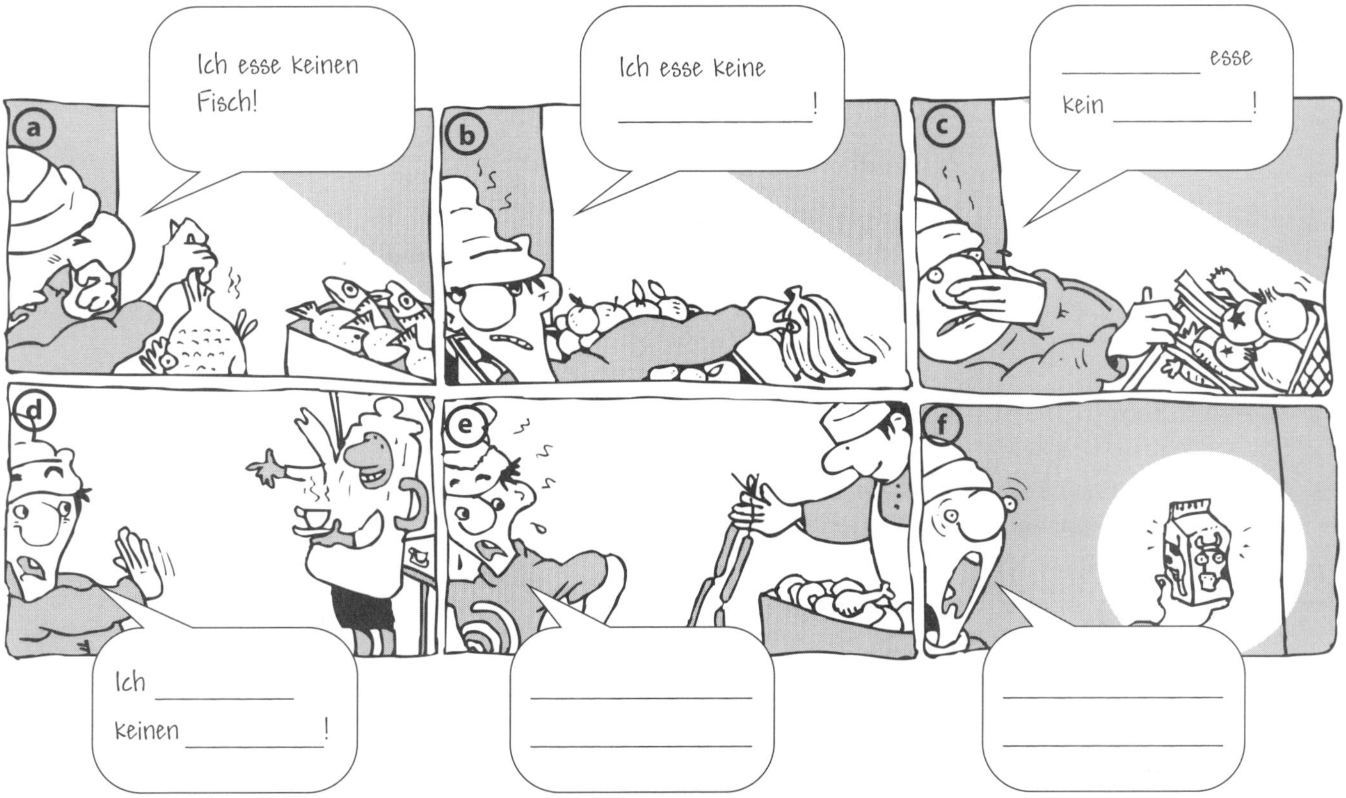

5.4 Koch mit!

1 **Schau das Bild an und kreuz die passenden Antworten an.**
Look at the picture and then tick the correct answers.

1 Jan macht …
- **a** Pizza mit Thunfisch. ☐
- **b** Currywurst. ☐
- **c** Pizza mit Wurst und Schinken. ☐

2 Mia isst …
- **a** kein Fleisch. ☐
- **b** kein Gemüse. ☐
- **c** keinen Fisch. ☐

3 Tims Lieblingsessen ist …
- **a** Pizza mit Tomaten. ☐
- **b** Nudeln mit Tomaten. ☐
- **c** Gemüse mit Schinken. ☐

2 **Cedi macht Nudelsalat. Was braucht er? Was braucht er nicht? Schreib ✓ oder ✗.**
What does Cedi need for pasta salad? Read the list and then tick or cross the boxes.

✗ Brötchen	☐ Marmelade	☐ Cornflakes
☐ Schinken	☐ Tomaten	☐ Nudeln
☐ Kaffee	☐ Orangensaft	☐ Käse
☐ Paprika	☐ Zwiebeln	☐ Tee

3 **Kathi macht ihre Lieblingspizza. Was braucht sie? Schreib eine Einkaufsliste für sie.**
Kathi is making her favourite pizza. Write a shopping list for her.

Tomaten

Grammatik 1

Flashback

Ich esse Obst.
→ Ich esse **gern** Obst.
→ Ich esse **nicht gern** Obst.

1 Schreib die Sätze richtig auf.
Write the sentences correctly.

a gern/Gemüseburger/esse/ich ______________________ .

b trinke/nicht/Milch/ich/gern ______________________ .

c Wasser/ich/gern/trinke ______________________ .

d nicht/esse/gern/ich/Fleisch ______________________ .

e ich/gern/Salat/esse/nicht ______________________ .

f gern/trinke/Kaffee/ich ______________________ .

2 Unterstreiche die passenden Wörter.
Underline the correct words.

a Ich trinke keinen/kein Orangensaft.

b Ich esse kein/keine Wurst.

c Ich trinke keine/keinen Tee.

d Ich esse kein/keine Cornflakes.

e Ich esse kein/keinen Gemüse.

f Ich trinke keine/kein Milch.

Flashback

masculine	→	Ich esse **keinen** Käse.
feminine	→	Ich trinke **keine** Milch.
neuter	→	Ich esse **kein** Brot.
plural	→	Ich esse **keine** Pommes frites.

3 Finde die passenden Bilder und füll die Lücken aus.
Find the correct pictures and fill in the gaps with **keinen/keine/kein.**

a

b

c

d

e

f

Ich trinke keinen Kaffee.

Ich esse __________ Käse.

Ich esse __________ Fleisch.

Ich trinke __________ Wasser.

Ich esse __________ Pommes frites.

Ich esse __________ Obst.

Grammatik 2

Flashback

	my	*your*	*his*	*her*	
masculine	mein	dein	sein	ihr	Jogurt
feminine	meine	deine	seine	ihre	Wurst
neuter	mein	dein	sein	ihr	Eis

1a Unterstreiche alle Maskulin-Wörter in Blau, alle Feminin-Wörter in Rot und alle Neutrum-Wörter in Grün.
Underline all masculine words in blue, all feminine words in red and all neuter words in green.

1 ein Salat
2 eine Pizza
3 ein Lehrer
4 eine Cola
5 ein Lieblingsessen
6 ein Lehrer

1b Schreib die Wörter in Übung 1a mit *mein/meine/mein* auf.
Write the words in activity 1a with mein/meine/mein.

1 ______________________

2 ______________________

3 ______________________

4 ______________________

5 ______________________

6 ______________________

1c Schreib die Wörter in Übung 1a mit *dein(e)/sein(e)/ihr(e)* auf.
Write the words in activity 1a with dein(e)/sein(e)/ihr(e).

Beispiel:

1 dein Salat (your)

2 ______________________ (her)

3 ______________________ (his)

4 ______________________ (your)

5 ______________________ (his)

6 ______________________ (her)

Ich esse/trinke …	***I'm eating/drinking …***
Was isst du?	*What are you eating?*
Was trinkst du?	*What are you drinking?*
Ich esse …	*I'm eating …*
einen Apfel	*an apple*
eine Banane	*a banana*
Brot/Brötchen	*bread/bread rolls*
Fisch	*fish*
ein Ei	*an egg*
Jogurt	*yoghurt*
Käse	*cheese*
Kartoffeln	*potatoes*
Nudeln	*pasta*
Salat	*salad*
Wurst	*sausage*
Ich trinke …	*I'm drinking …*
Cola	*coke*
Milch	*milk*
Orangensaft	*orange juice*

Mahlzeiten	***Meals***
Wass isst du …	*What do you eat …*
zum Frühstück?	*for breakfast?*
zum Mittagessen?	*for lunch?*
zum Abendessen?	*for dinner?*
Ich esse normalerweise Brot.	*I usually eat bread.*
Ich esse meistens Nudeln.	*I mainly eat pasta.*
Zum Frühstück esse ich …	*For breakfast I eat …*
Cornflakes/Müsli	*cornflakes/muesli*
Brot mit Marmelade	*bread with jam*
Brötchen mit Honig	*bread rolls with honey*
Zum Mittagessen esse ich ...	*For lunch I eat ...*
Hähnchen mit Reis	*chicken with rice*
Zum Abendessen esse ich ...	*For dinner I eat ...*
Brot mit Butter und Käse	*bread with butter and cheese*
Was trinkst du …	*What do you drink …*
zum Frühstück/Mittagessen/Abendessen?	*for breakfast/lunch/dinner?*
Zum Frühstück trinke ich Kaffee.	*For breakfast I drink coffee.*
Zum Mittagessen trinke ich Wasser.	*For lunch I drink water.*
Zum Abendessen trinke ich Tee.	*For dinner I drink tea.*

Was isst/trinkst du gern?	***What do you like to eat/drink?***
Was isst du gern?	*What do you like to eat?*
Was trinkst du gern?	*What do you like to drink?*
Was isst du nicht gern?	*What don't you like to eat?*
Was trinkst du nicht gern?	*What don't you like to drink?*
Ich esse (nicht) gern …	*I (don't) like to eat …*
Fleisch	*meat*
Gemüse	*vegetables*
Obst	*fruit*
Pommes frites	*fries/chips*
Ich trinke (nicht) gern …	*I (don't) like to drink …*
Kaffee	*coffee*
Milch	*milk*
Ich esse …	*I …*
keinen Fisch	*don't eat fish*
keine Wurst	*don't eat sausage*
kein Gemüse	*don't eat vegetables*
keine Pommes frites	*don't eat fries/chips*
Ich trinke …	*I …*
keinen Kaffee	*don't drink coffee*
keine Milch	*don't drink milk*
kein Wasser	*don't drink water*

Kochen	***Cooking***
Ich mache Pizza mit …	*I'm making a pizza with …*
Ei	*egg*
Paprika	*peppers*
Pilzen	*mushrooms*
Schinken	*ham*
Thunfisch	*tuna*
Wurst	*sausage*
Man braucht …	*You need …*
Käse	*cheese*
Pilze	*mushrooms*
Spinat	*spinach*
Tomaten	*tomatoes*
Zwiebeln	*onions*
Mein Lieblingsessen ist …	*My favourite food is …*
Pizza mit Thunfisch	*pizza with tuna*

Kannst du …? Checklist

This is a checklist of the things you should aim to learn in German using Klasse! neu 1.
Use the **Check** boxes and the **Prove it!** column to keep track of what you have learned.

- Tick the first box when you feel you are getting to grips with the learning objective, but sometimes need a prompt or time to think.
- Tick the second box when you think you have fully mastered the learning objective and will be able to use it again in future.
- Make notes following the prompts in the **Prove it!** column to help you show what you have learned. Your learning partner or parent can test you and initial the second box to confirm the progress you have made.

Learning objectives	**Check**		**Prove it!**
I can say what I eat and drink.	☐	☐	*Get partner to test you.*
I can say what I don't eat and drink.	☐	☐	*Get partner to test you.*
I can say what I eat and drink for different meals.	☐	☐	*Get partner to test you.*
I can ask someone what he/she eats and drinks for different meals.	☐	☐	*Get partner to test you.*
I can say when I eat and drink different meals.	☐	☐	*Get partner to test you.*
I can ask someone when he/she eats and drinks different meals.	☐	☐	*Get partner to test you.*
I can say what I like and don't like to eat and drink.	☐	☐	*Get partner to test you.*
I can ask someone what he/she likes to eat and drink.	☐	☐	*Get partner to test you.*
I can talk about my favourite food.	☐	☐	*Get partner to test you.*
I can talk about my favourite recipes.	☐	☐	*Get partner to test you.*
I can use the German–English section of a dictionary.	☐	☐	*Find the English for these words:* Mittagessen, Kartoffeln, Wurst.
I can use the English–German section of a dictionary.	☐	☐	*Find the German for these words: pear, cake, onions.*
I can use *mein, dein, sein, ihr* with the right endings.	☐	☐	*How do you say:* *'That's my milk!'* *'What's her favourite ice cream?'* *'Is that your salad?'* *in German?*
I can recognize the difference in sounds between a long and a short *o* and a long and a short *u*.	☐	☐	*Say these words aloud:* Limonade, Honig, Hunger, Nudeln.

Was spielst du gern?

1 **Schreib die Wörter richtig auf.**
Write the jumbled-up words correctly.

a NSTNIE ______________________

b XOSANOF ______________________

c RETIGRA ______________________

d POMTREET ______________________

e ABLUFßL ______________________

f UBYGR ______________________

2 **Was spielst du? Füll die Lücken aus.**
Fill in the gaps in the speech bubbles.

Ich spiele …

a

b

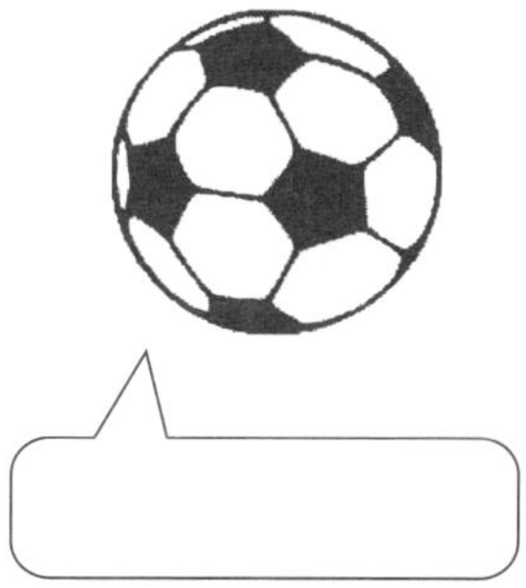

c

d

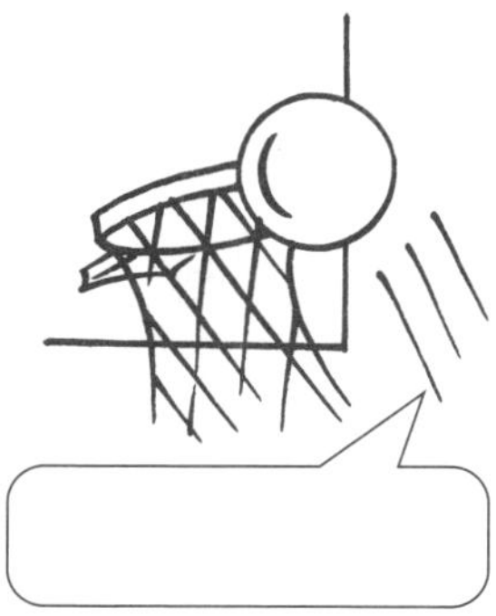

e

f

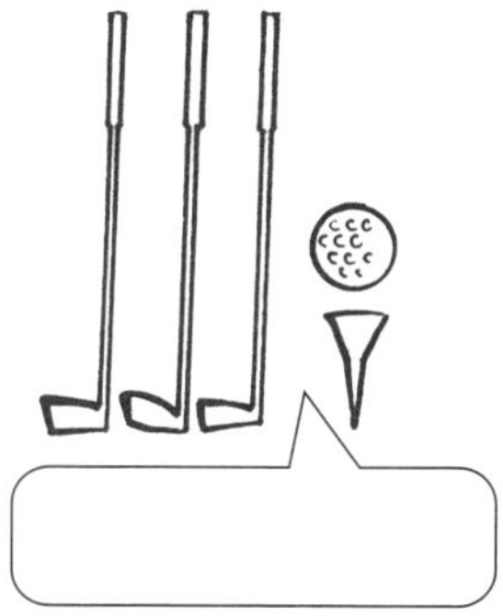

g

h

i

6.2 Hobbys

1 **Finde die passenden Wörter.**
Draw a line to show the end of each sentence.

1	Ich fahre	**a**	Musik.
2	Ich spiele	**b**	im Internet.
3	Ich surfe	**c**	fern.
4	Ich höre	**d**	Rollschuh.
5	Ich sehe	**e**	Karten.

2 **Finde die passenden Bilder.**
Draw lines to match the pictures to the sentences.

a

b

c

d

e

f

1 Ich reite nicht gern.

2 Ich tanze gern.

3 Ich fahre gern Rad.

4 Ich schwimme nicht gern.

5 Ich spiele nicht gern Karten.

6 Ich fahre gern Skateboard.

Ich sehe gern fern!

1 **Was für eine Sendung ist das? Schreib die passenden Wörter auf.**
Write the correct words for the TV programmes.

a

eine ________________

b

eine ________________

c

ein ________________

d

eine ________________

e

die ________________

f

eine ________________

2 **Schreib die Sätze richtig auf.**
Find four sentences and write them down.

ichfindeSportsendungeninteressantichsehenichtgernNachrichtenichfindeTrickfilmedoofmeineLieblingssendungistMarienhof

Ich finde ... ____

____

____

____

Wie oft machst du …?

1 **Schreib die Sätze richtig auf.**
Write the sentences correctly.

a b c d e

a Einmal pro Woche ____________ ____________ Tennis.

b Nachmittags ____________ ich ____________ .

c Am Wochenende ____________ ____________ ____________ .

d Jeden Morgen ____________ ____________ .

e Jeden Abend ____________ ____________ ____________ .

2 **Was macht Maxi-Monster wann? Schreib Sprechblasen.**
What does Maxi-Monster do when? Write sentences.

Grammatik 1

Flashback

The present tense endings of regular verbs follow this pattern:

schreiben
ich schreib**e**
du schreib**st**
er/sie/es schreib**t**
wir schreib**en**
ihr schreib**t**
sie/Sie schreib**en**

1 **Füll die Lücken für *finden* aus.**
***Fill in the correct verb endings for* finden.**

a ich find_______
b du find_______
c er/sie/es find_______
d wir find_______
e ihr_______
f sie/Sie _______

2 **Füll die Lücken aus.**
Fill in the verb endings.

a Wir schreib_____ eine E-Mail.

b Er heiß_____ Kai.

c Sie spiel_____ Tennis.

d Ich mach_____ Pizza.

e Kauf_____ ihr ein Eis?

f Wo wohn_____ du?

Grammatik 2

Flashback

Some irregular verbs also change their spellings in the *du* and *er/sie/es* forms:

	lesen	**sehen**	**fahren**
ich	lese	sehe	fahre
du	**lie**st	**sie**hst	f**ä**hrst
er/sie/es	**lie**st	**sie**ht	f**ä**hrt
		e → ie	**a → ä**

1 Finde sechs Sätze.

Draw lines to join the beginnings and ends of sentences.

a Ich	**1** fährt nicht gern Rad.
b Du	**2** lese eine E-Mail.
c Er	**3** seht abends fern.
d Wir	**4** liest gern.
e Ihr	**5** fahren Skateboard.
f Sie	**6** sehen nicht gern fern.

2 Finde die passenden Bilder.

Draw lines to match the picture to the correct speech bubble.

1

2

3

a Du fährst gern Rollschuh.

b Ich lese nicht gern.

c Wir sehen gern fern.

d Er fährt morgens Rad.

e Du liest einen Brief.

f Sie sieht gern Seifenopern.

4

5

6

Was spielst du gern?	***What do you like playing?***
Was spielst du gern?	*What do you like playing?*
Ich spiele gern …	*I like playing …*
Basketball/Fußball/Golf/Tennis/Volleyball/Rugby/Klavier/Geige/Gitarre/Trompete/Saxofon/Schlagzeug	*basketball/football/golf/tennis/volleyball/rugby/piano/violin/guitar/trumpet/saxophone/drums*

Hobbys	***Hobbies***
Was ist dein Hobby?	*What's your hobby?*
Was sind deine Hobbys?	*What are your hobbies?*
Ich lese. / Ich reite./Ich schwimme.	*I read. / I ride. / I swim.*
Ich tanze.	*I dance.*
Ich spiele …	*I play …*
Computerspiele	*computer games*
Karten	*cards*
Ich fahre Skateboard/Rad/Rollschuh.	*I go skateboarding/cycling/rollerskating.*
Ich höre Musik.	*I listen to music.*
Ich surfe im Internet.	*I surf the Internet.*

Fernsehen	***TV***
Was für eine Sendung ist das?	*What kind of programme is that?*
Das ist …	*That is …*
ein Film	*a film*
ein Dokumentarfilm	*a documentary*
ein Trickfilm	*a cartoon film*
eine Musiksendung	*a music programme*
eine Talkshow	*a talk show*
eine Seifenoper	*a soap opera*
eine Serie	*a series*
eine Sportsendung	*a sports programme*
Das sind die Nachrichten.	*That's the news.*
Wie findest du Filme?	*What do you think of films?*
Siehst du gern Serien?	*Do you like watching series?*
Was ist deine Lieblingssendung?	*What's your favourite programme?*
Ich finde …	*I find …*
Das ist …	*That's …*
lustig/spannend	*funny/exciting*
interessant	*interesting*
blöd/doof	*stupid*
langweilig	*boring*
Ich sehe (nicht) gern …	*I (don't) like watching …*
Meine Lieblingssendung ist …	*My favourite programme is …*

Wie oft/wann?	***How often/when?***
Wie spät ist es?	*What time is it?*
Was machst du um … Uhr?	*What are you doing at … o'clock?*
Wie oft machst du Sport?	*How often do you do sport?*
Wie oft spielst du Karten?	*How often do you play cards?*
Wie oft siehst du fern?	*How often do you watch TV?*
jeden Tag	*every day*
jeden Morgen	*every morning*
jeden Nachmittag	*every afternoon*
jeden Abend	*every evening*
morgens	*in the morning*
nachmittags	*in the afternoon*
abends	*in the evening*
am Wochenende	*at the weekend*
am Montag	*on Monday*
einmal pro Woche	*once a week*
zweimal pro Monat	*twice a month*

Kannst du …? Checklist

This is a checklist of the things you should aim to learn in German using Klasse! neu 1.
Use the **Check** boxes and the **Prove it!** column to keep track of what you have learned.

- ★ Tick the first box when you feel you are getting to grips with the learning objective, but sometimes need a prompt or time to think.
- ★ Tick the second box when you think you have fully mastered the learning objective and will be able to use it again in future.
- ★ Make notes following the prompts in the **Prove it!** column to help you show what you have learned. Your learning partner or parent can test you and initial the second box to confirm the progress you have made.

Learning objectives	**Check**		**Prove it!**
I can say which sports and musical instruments I play.	☐	☐	*Get partner to test you.*
I can talk about my hobbies.	☐	☐	*Get partner to test you.*
I can ask someone about his/her hobbies.	☐	☐	*Get partner to test you.*
I can say what I like/don't like doing.	☐	☐	*Get partner to test you.*
I can ask someone what he/she likes/doesn't like doing.	☐	☐	*Get partner to test you.*
I can ask about TV programmes.	☐	☐	*Get partner to test you.*
I can describe TV programmes.	☐	☐	*Get partner to test you.*
I can ask for and give opinions about TV programmes.	☐	☐	*Get partner to test you.*
I can say when and how often I do something.	☐	☐	*Get partner to test you.*
I can ask someone about when and how often he/she does something.	☐	☐	*Get partner to test you.*
I can form the present tense of regular verbs.	☐	☐	*Ask your partner three questions about hobbies.*
I can use the correct word order with time expressions at the beginning of a sentence.	☐	☐	*Explain to a partner.*
I can recognize the different sounds *sp* and *sch*.	☐	☐	*Say these words aloud:* Sport, Schule, spricht, schreibt.

Woher kommst du?

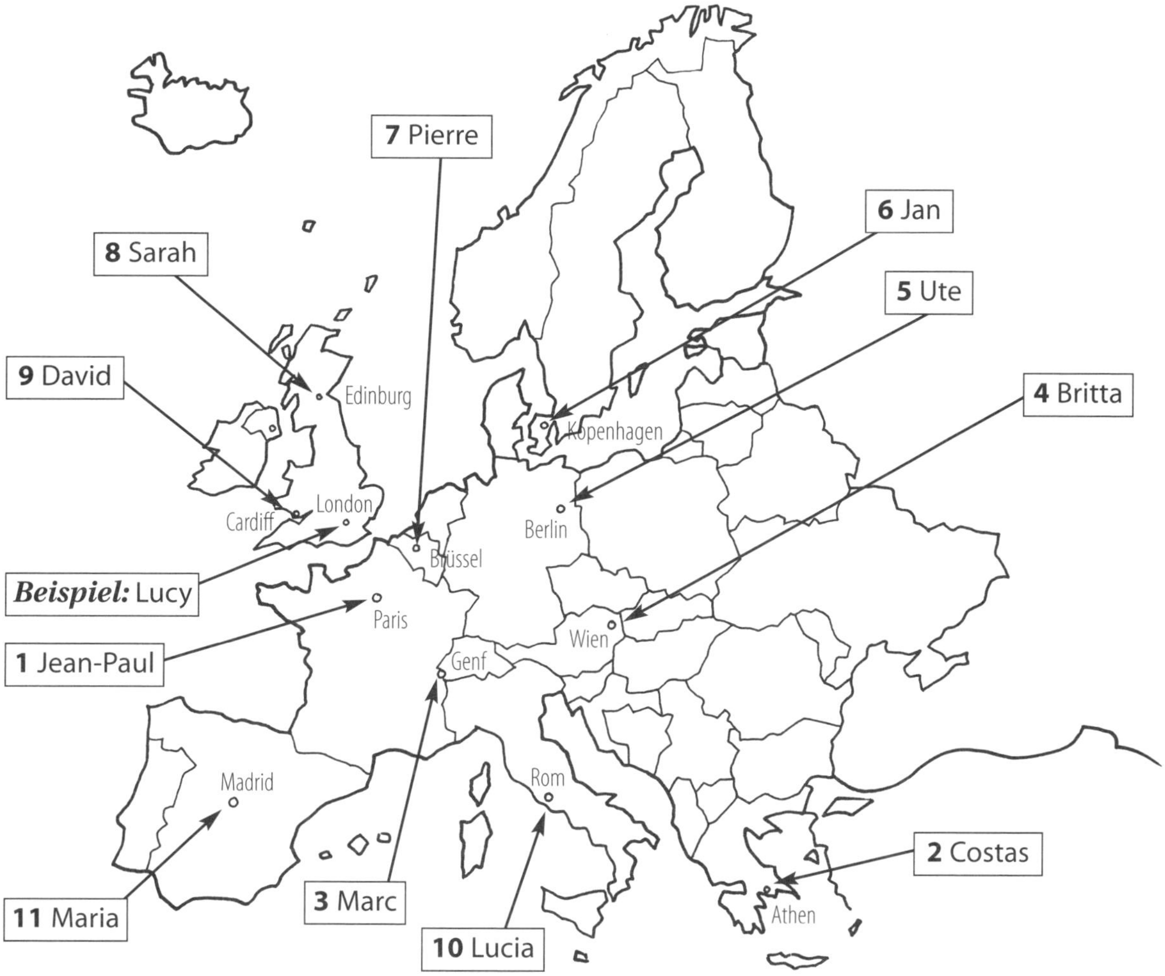

~~England~~
Schottland
Wales
Deutschland
Österreich
die Schweiz
Frankreich
Belgien
Spanien
Italien
Griechenland
Dänemark

1 **Wo wohnen diese Jugendlichen? Schreib Sätze.**
Where do these teenagers live? Write sentences.

Beispiel: *Lucy: Ich komme aus England. Ich wohne in London. Das ist im Süden.*

1 ______
2 ______
3 ______
4 ______
5 ______
6 ______
7 ______
8 ______
9 ______
10 ______
11 ______

Was gibt es in Hollfeld?

1 Worträtsel. Schreib die Wörter auf.

Fill in the missing places to complete the puzzle and find a new word.

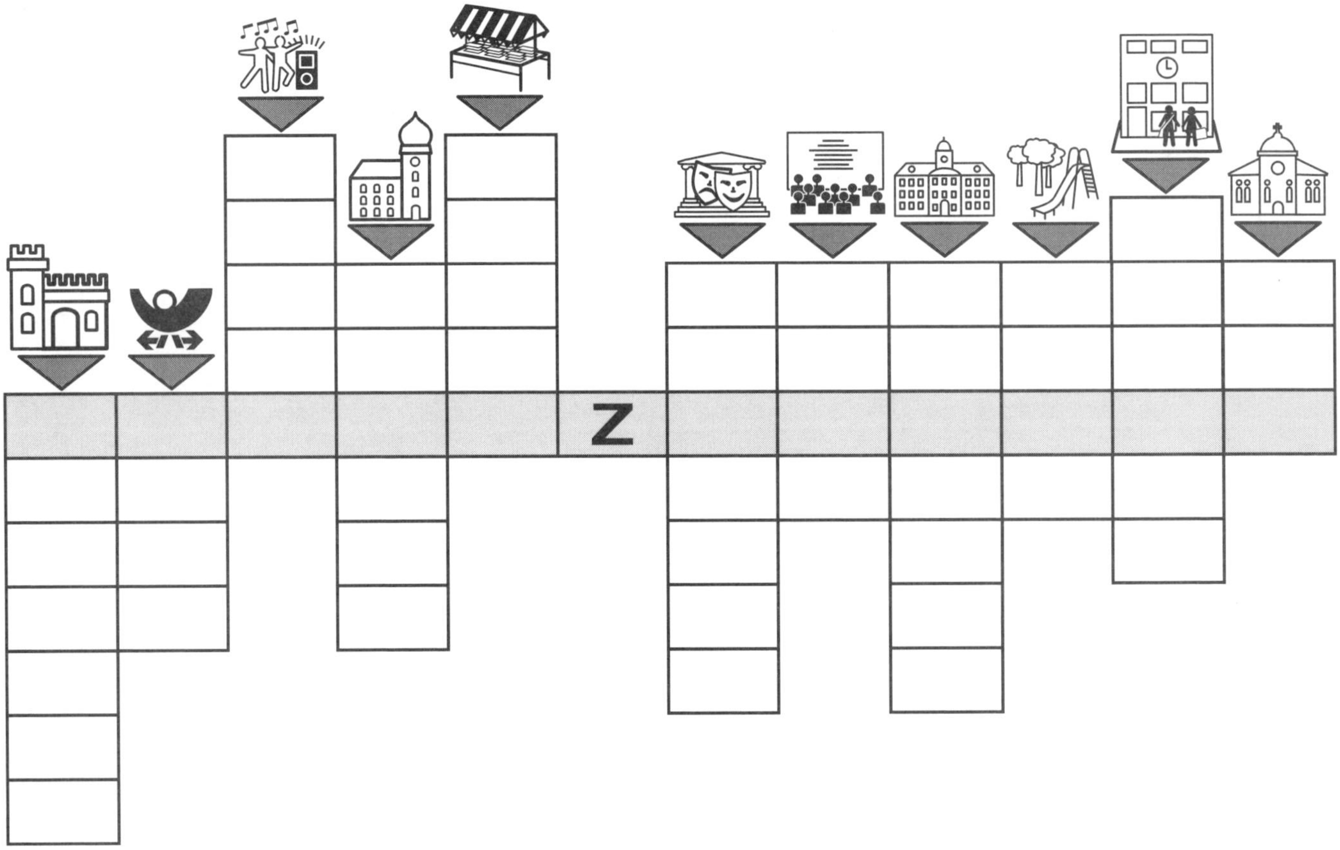

2 Lies Tanjas E-Mail. Richtig oder falsch?

Read Tanja's e-mail. True or false?

	R	F
a Mössingen ist eine kleine Stadt.	☐	☐
b Mössingen liegt im Norden.	☐	☐
c Das Schwimmbad ist modern.	☐	☐
d Es gibt kein Kino.	☐	☐
e Der Markt ist sehr gut.	☐	☐
f Die Kirche ist alt.	☐	☐
g Es gibt ein interessantes Museum.	☐	☐

Hallo! Ich bin Tanja und ich wohne in Mössingen in Deutschland. Mössingen ist eine kleine Stadt im Südwesten in der Nähe von Stuttgart. In Mössingen gibt es ein modernes Schwimmbad und ein kleines Kino. Es gibt auch einen tollen Markt am Samstag und einen schönen Park. Wir haben auch eine alte Kirche und ein neues Rathaus, aber kein Museum und keine Disco – schade!

Was kann man hier machen?

1 Finde die passenden Bilder.

Draw lines to match up the sentences to the correct pictures.

1 Man kann ins Jugendzentrum gehen.
2 Man kann ins Museum gehen.
3 Man kann einen Einkaufsbummel machen.
4 Man kann ins Sportzentrum gehen.
5 Man kann ins Fastfood-Restaurant gehen.
6 Man kann ins Popkonzert gehen.
7 Man kann ins Schwimmbad gehen.
8 Man kann auf die Eisbahn gehen.
9 Man kann ins Kino gehen.
10 Man kann ein Picknick machen.

a 

b 

c 

d 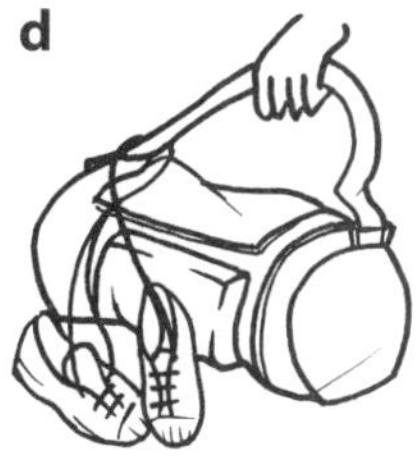

e 

f 

g 

h 

i 

j 

2 Was kann man in Stuttgart machen? Schreib Sätze.

Write sentences to describe what you can do in Stuttgart.

a  ______________________________

b  ______________________________

c  ______________________________

d  ______________________________

e 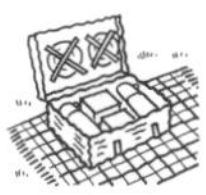 ______________________________

f  ______________________________

Wie fährst du in die Stadt?

1 Schreib die Sätze richtig auf.

Write the sentences in the correct order.

1 [Auto] [fahre] [mit] [Ich] [dem] [.] Ich fahre mit dem Auto.

2 [mit] [Fährst] [der] [du] [U-Bahn] [?] ____________

3 [dem] [Wir] [Zug] [mit] [fahren] [.] ____________

4 [Fuß] [gehe] [zu] [Ich] [.] ____________

5 [der] [mit] [du] [Straßenbahn] [Fährst] [?] ____________

6 [Wir] [Rad] [dem] [fahren] [mit] [.] ____________

7 [mit] [Bus] [Ich] [dem] [fahre] [.] ____________

2 Finde jetzt die passenden Bilder für die Sätze in Übung 1.

Find the matching pictures for the sentences in activity 1.

a  [ ]

b 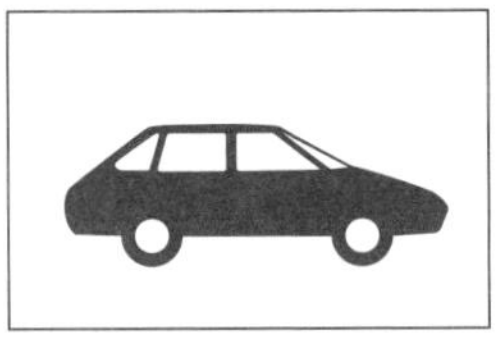 [1]

c  [ ]

d 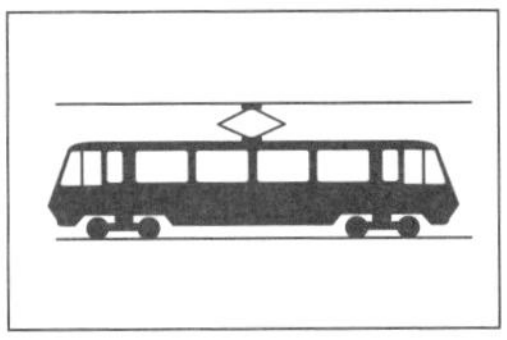 [ ]

e  [ ]

f  [ ]

g  [ ]

3 Was macht Angelika am Samstag? Richtig oder falsch?

What does Angelika do on Saturdays? True or false?

Es ist Samstag und ich fahre mit dem Bus in die Stadt – eine Fahrkarte hin und zurück kostet zwei Euro zwanzig. Das ist NICHT billig! In der Stadt kaufe ich CDs. Ich gehe nachmittags zu Fuß mit Katja zum Sportzentrum. Und abends? Wir gehen in die Disco oder ins Kino.

	Richtig	Falsch
1 Angelika fährt mit dem Bus in die Stadt.	✗	
2 Die Fahrkarte ist teuer.		
3 Sie kauft Bücher.		
4 Sie geht mit Karl zum Sportzentrum.		
5 Sie gehen zu Fuß.		
6 Am Samstagabend gehen sie ins Theater.		

Grammatik 1

Flashback

der Bahnhof → Es gibt **einen** Bahnhof.
die Bank → Es gibt **eine** Bank.
das Theater → Es gibt **ein** Theater.

1 Was gibt es in dieser Stadt?
Describe what there is in this town.

ein kleines Sportzentrum | eine neue Schule | einen kleinen Bahnhof | einen schönen Park | ein kleines Kino | eine moderne Kirche | einen großen Bahnhof | eine alte Kirche | ein modernes Sportzentrum

Es gibt …

____

____

____

2 Füll die Lücken aus.
Fill in the gaps.

In meiner Stadt gibt es ein____ toll____ Markt, ein____ groß____ Bank, ein____ schön____ Dom, ein____ modern____ Theater, ein____ alt____ Bahnhof, ein____ toll____ Sportzentrum und ein____ alt____ Rathaus.

Grammatik 2

Flashback

der Park → Ich fahre mit dem Bus **zum** Park.
die Schule → Ich fahre mit der Straßenbahn **zur** Schule.
das Schwimmbad → Ich fahre mit dem Rad **zum** Schwimmbad.

1 *zum* **oder** *zur*? **Schreib die Wörter auf.**
zum *or* zur? *Write the words in the box in the correct place.*

ZUM ⟷ ZUR

Schule

~~Schule~~ Kirche Rathaus Sportzentrum Disco Kino Bank
Schloss Park Markt Hallenbad Dom Bahnhof

2 **Wohin fahren sie und wie? Schreib Sätze.**
Where are they going and how? Write sentences.

	Dieter				
					Frau Haab
			Sabina		
				Mustafa	
					Herr Albrecht
		Sven			

Beispiel: *Mustafa fährt mit dem Bus zum Schwimmbad.*

Woher kommst du?	***Where do you come from?***
Ich komme aus ...	*I come from ...*
England	*England*
Schottland	*Scotland*
Irland	*Ireland*
Wales	*Wales*
Deutschland	*Germany*
Österreich	*Austria*
der Schweiz	*Switzerland*
Frankreich	*France*
Belgien	*Belgium*
Holland	*Holland*
Spanien	*Spain*
Italien	*Italy*
Portugal	*Portugal*
Griechenland	*Greece*
Dänemark	*Denmark*
im Norden	*in the north*
im Süden	*in the south*
im Westen	*in the west*
im Osten	*in the east*
im Nordosten	*in the north-east*
im Nordwesten	*in the north-west*
im Südosten	*in the south-east*
im Südwesten	*in the south-west*

Willkommen in Hollfeld	***Welcome to Hollfeld***
der Bahnhof	*the station*
der Dom	*the cathedral*
der Markt	*the market*
der Park	*the park*
die Bank	*the bank*
die Disco	*the disco*
die Kirche	*the church*
die Post	*the post office*
das Hallenbad	*the (indoor) swimming-pool*
das Schwimmbad	*the (outdoor) swimming-pool*
das Kino	*the cinema*
das Rathaus	*the town hall*
das Schloss	*the castle*
das Sportzentrum	*the sports centre*
das Theater	*the theatre*
modern	*modern*
neu	*new*
alt	*old*
interessant	*interesting*
groß	*big*
toll	*great, super*
schön	*beautiful*
klein	*small*

Was kann man in Bayreuth machen?	***What can you do in Bayreuth?***
Man kann ...	*You can ...*
ins Museum gehen	*go to the museum*
ins Jugendzentrum gehen	*go to the youth centre*
einen Einkaufsbummel machen	*go shopping*
ins Sportzentrum gehen	*go to the sports centre*
ins Fast-food Restaurant gehen.	*go to a fast food restaurant.*
ins Popkonzert gehen	*go to a pop concert*
ins Schwimmbad gehen	*go to the (outdoor) swimming-pool*
ins Hallenbad gehen	*go to the (indoor) swimming-pool*
auf die Eisbahn gehen	*go to the ice rink*
ins Kino gehen	*go to the cinema*
ein Picknick machen	*have a picnic*
das Schloss besuchen	*visit the castle*

Wie fährst du in die Stadt?	***How do you travel to town?***
Ich fahre ...	*I travel ...*
mit dem Bus	*by bus*
mit dem Auto	*by car*
mit dem Zug	*by train*
mit dem Rad	*by bike*
mit der U-Bahn	*by underground*
mit der Straßenbahn	*by tram*
Ich gehe zu Fuß	*I walk*

Kannst du …? Checklist

This is a checklist of the things you should aim to learn in German using Klasse! neu 1.
Use the **Check** boxes and the **Prove it!** column to keep track of what you have learned.

- ★ Tick the first box when you feel you are getting to grips with the learning objective, but sometimes need a prompt or time to think.
- ★ Tick the second box when you think you have fully mastered the learning objective and will be able to use it again in future.
- ★ Make notes following the prompts in the **Prove it!** column to help you show what you have learned. Your learning partner or parent can test you and initial the second box to confirm the progress you have made.

Learning objectives	**Check**		**Prove it!**
I can say the names of different European countries.	☐	☐	*Get partner to test you.*
I can say which country I come from.	☐	☐	*Get partner to test you.*
I can describe where my town is.	☐	☐	*Get partner to test you.*
I can ask where somebody comes from.	☐	☐	*Get partner to test you.*
I can describe the public buildings in my town or village.	☐	☐	*Get partner to test you.*
I can describe what the town and buildings are like.	☐	☐	*Get partner to test you.*
I can use the correct endings for adjectives after *Es gibt …*	☐	☐	*Without looking at the book, write down 'There is a beautiful cathedral, a modern sports centre and an old church'.*
I can say what activities you can do in a town.	☐	☐	*Get partner to test you.*
I can ask which means of transport someone uses.	☐	☐	*Get partner to test you.*
I can say which means of transport I use.	☐	☐	*Get partner to test you.*
I can say where I am going.	☐	☐	*Get partner to test you.*
I can recognize the different sounds *s, ß, sch, st.*	☐	☐	*Say these words aloud:* Schule, super, Stadt, Fuß.
I can recognize the different sounds *ü, ö.*	☐	☐	*Say these words aloud:* Göttingen, Übung, öffnen, Überlingen

8.1 Wie ist das Wetter?

1 Finde die passenden Bilder.

Match up the weather phrases to the correct picture.

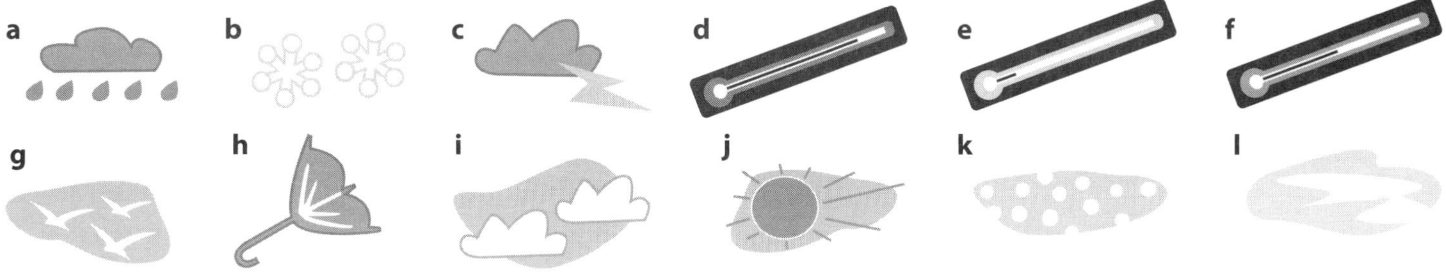

1 Es ist sonnig.	**2** Es regnet.	**3** Es ist schön.	**4** Es ist heiß.
5 Es ist kalt.	**6** Es ist frostig.	**7** Es schneit.	**8** Es gewittert.
9 Es ist neblig.	**10** Es ist bewölkt.	**11** Es ist warm.	**12** Es ist windig.

2a Lies den Wetterbericht. Welche Karte ist das? A oder B?

Read the weather report. Which map is it describing?

A

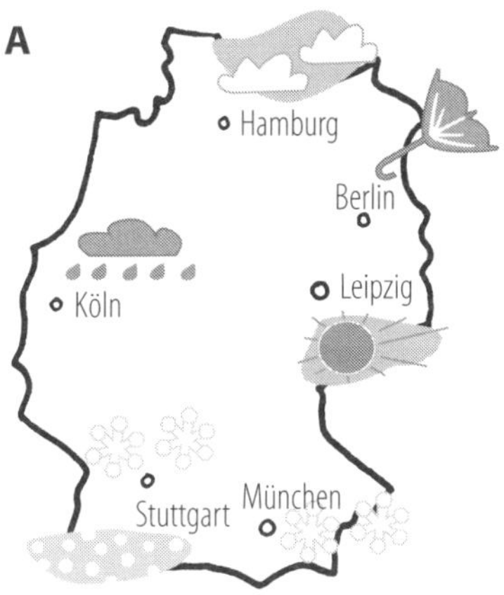

B

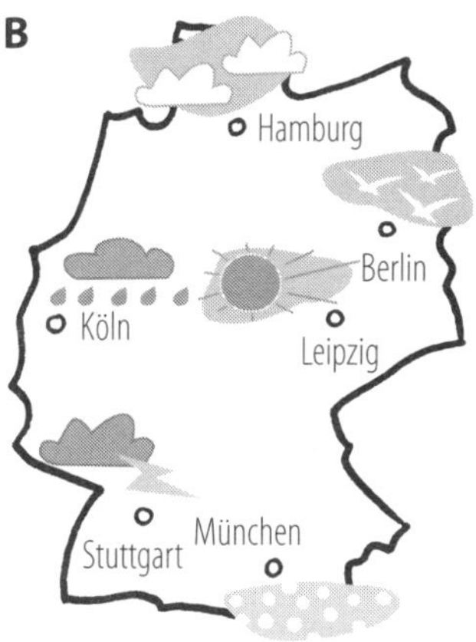

Heute ist es sonnig in Leipzig, aber nicht in Berlin: es ist windig. In München ist es frostig. In Stuttgart ist es auch frostig und es schneit. Es regnet in Köln und in Hamburg ist es auch nicht schön. In Hamburg ist es bewölkt.

2b Schreib den Wetterbericht für die andere Karte.

Write the weather report for the other map.

München In München schneit es.

Köln ______________________

Hamburg ______________________

Berlin ______________________

Leipzig ______________________

Stuttgart ______________________

Was machen wir?

1 **Ersetze die Bilder mit Wörtern.**
Replace the pictures with words.

a Willst du  ins Kino gehen ?

b Willst du 

_______________?

c Willst du 

_______________?

d Willst du  _______________?

e Willst du  _______________?

in die Stadt gehen	~~ins Kino gehen~~	Basketball spielen	zum Park gehen	einen Einkaufsbummel machen

2 **Wann und wo treffen sie sich? Schreib Sätze.**
When and where are they meeting? Write sentences.

a 

Wir treffen uns um sieben Uhr am Rathaus.

b  _______________

c  _______________

d  _______________

e 

____

f 

____

3 **Bring den Dialog in die richtige Reihenfolge.**
Put the conversation in the correct order.

Hallo, Anna, hier Max. [1] Gut, danke. Willst du morgen ins Kino gehen? [ ]
Um sieben Uhr an der Post. [ ] Tschüs. [ ] Hallo, Max. Wie geht's? [ ]
Ja, tolle Idee. Wann treffen wir uns? [ ] Prima, bis dann. [ ]

Im Supermarkt

1 **Wie viel Geld ist das? Finde die passenden Wörter.**
How much? Match the prices to the right picture.

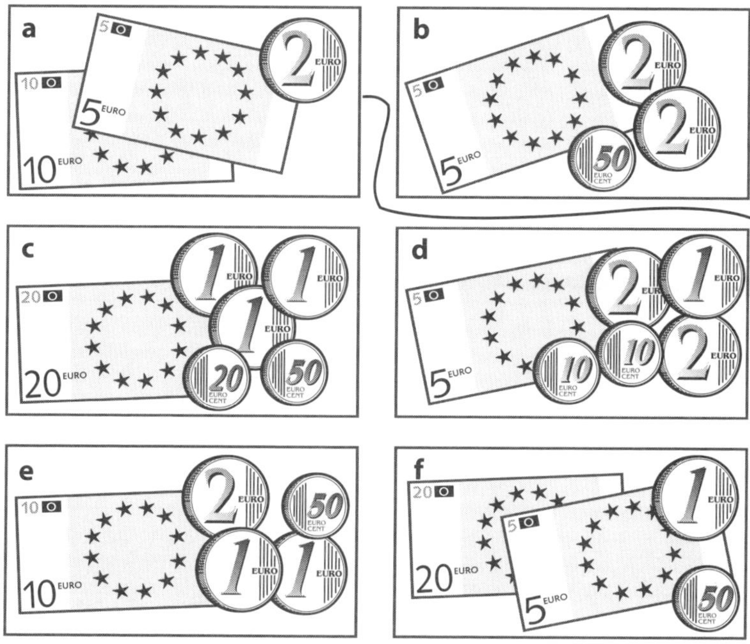

1 zehn Euro zwanzig

2 vierzehn Euro fünfzig

3 neun Euro fünfzig

4 siebzehn Euro

5 sechsundzwanzig Euro fünfzig

6 dreiundzwanzig Euro siebzig

2a **Lies die Broschüre und schreib die Preise auf.**
Read the brochure and write in the correct prices.

a eine Dose Cola
b ____________________
c ____________________
d ____________________
e ____________________
f ____________________
g ____________________
h ____________________

2b **Schreib eine Einkaufsliste.**
Write a shopping list.

Im Café

1 Was bestellen sie?

What are these people ordering? Fill in the speech bubbles.

a

b

c

d

e

f

ein Käsebrot   ein Vanilleeis   einen Orangensaft   ~~eine Limonade~~
einen Hamburger mit Pommes   eine heiße Schokolade mit Sahne

2 Lies das Gesprach und wähle die richtigen Bilder.

Read the conversation and tick the pictures that are mentioned.

Kellner: Guten Tag.
Kunde: Guten Tag. Ich möchte ein Käsebrot, bitte.
Kellner: Und zu trinken?
Kunde: Zu trinken nehme ich einen Orangensaft.
Kellner: Gut, ist das alles?
Kunde: Ich möchte auch ein Vanilleeis.
Kellner: Danke, kommt sofort.

a

☐

b

☐

c

☐

d

☐

e

☐

f

☐

Grammatik 1

Flashback

Wenn es sonnig **ist**, **spiele** ich Tennis.

verb — comma — verb

1 Finde die passsenden Bilder.

Match the speech bubbles to the correct pictures.

a

b

c

d

e

f

1 Wenn es heiß ist, fahre ich Rad.

2 Wenn es schön ist, spiele ich Tennis.

3 Wenn es regnet, gehe ich zum Sportzentrum.

4 Wenn es schneit, fahre ich Ski.

5 Wenn es sonnig ist, spiele ich Fußball.

6 Wenn es kalt ist, gehe ich ins Kino.

2 Füll die Lücken aus.

Fill in the gaps.

a Wenn es sonnig ________, ________ ich ________.

gehe | schwimmen | ist

b Wenn ________ ________ ist, gehe ________ ________.

Windsurfen | es | windig | ich

c Wenn ________ ________ ________, ________ ________ ins Kino.

kalt | gehe | ich | es | ist

d Wenn ________ ________ ________, ________ ________ Tennis.

spiele | es | ist | sonnig | ich

Grammatik 2

1 **Füll die Lücken mit der richtigen Form von *wollen* aus.**
Fill the gaps with the correct form of wollen.

a Ich ____________ ins Kino gehen.

b ______________ du auf die Eisbahn gehen?

c Jana ____________ einen Einkaufsbummel machen.

d Oliver und Daniel ___________ schwimmen gehen.

e Was ____________ ihr machen?

f Wir ______________ ins Sportzentrum gehen.

g ______________ Sie ins Museum gehen?

wollen will will willst
wollt wollen wollen

Flashback

wollen
ich will
du willst
er/sie/es will
wir wollen
ihr wollt
Sie wollen
sie wollen

2 **Füll die Lücken mit der richtigen Form von *können* aus.**
Fill the gaps with the correct form of können.

a Wir __________________ ein Picknick machen.

b _____________ du schwimmen? Ich _________ nicht schwimmen.

c ______________ ihr Tennis spielen?

d Thomas __________ nicht Ski fahren.

e Anja und Ute __________ sehr gut Basketball spielen.

f _____________ Sie Basketball spielen?

können kann kannst können
kann können könnt

Flashback

können
ich kann
du kannst
er/sie es kann
wir können
ihr könnt
Sie können
sie können

3 **Welche Frage passt zu welcher Antwort?**
Draw lines to match the questions and answers.

1 Was wollt ihr machen?
2 Was willst du machen?
3 Was willst du essen?
4 Was willst du trinken?
5 Willst du Tennis spielen?

a Eine Pizza.
b Nein, danke. Ich kann nicht Tennis spielen.
c Einen Orangensaft.
d Wir wollen schwimmen gehen.
e Ich will auf die Eisbahn gehen.

Wie ist das Wetter?	***What is the weather like?***
Es ist sonnig.	*It's sunny.*
Es regnet.	*It's raining.*
Es ist schön.	*It's fine.*
Es ist heiß.	*It's hot.*
Es ist kalt.	*It's cold.*
Es ist frostig.	*It's frosty.*
Es schneit.	*It's snowing.*
Es gewittert.	*There's thunder and lightning.*
Es ist neblig.	*It's foggy.*
Es ist bewölkt.	*It's cloudy.*
Es ist warm.	*It's warm.*
Es ist windig.	*it's windy.*
Wenn es regnet, gehe ich zum Sportzentrum.	*When it rains, I go to the sports centre.*

Was machen wir?	***What shall we do?***
Ich will zum Park gehen.	*I want to go to the park.*
Wir können ins Sportzentrum gehen.	*We can go to the sports centre.*
Was willst du machen?	*What do you want to do?*
Wann und wo treffen wir uns?	*When and where shall we meet?*
Wir treffen uns um drei Uhr an der Post.	*Let's meet at 3 o'clock at the post office.*

Im Supermarkt	***In the supermarket***
Was darf es sein?	*What would you like?*
Was kostet das?	*What does that cost?*
Das kostet ...	*It costs ...*
ein Euro vierzig	*one euro forty*
zwei Euro achtzig	*two euros eighty*
sechzig Cent	*60 cents*
ein Kilo	*a kilo*
500 Gramm	*500 grammes*
eine Packung	*a packet*
eine Flasche	*a bottle*
eine Dose	*a can*
eine Tüte	*a bag*
ein Becher	*a tub*
ein Liter	*a litre*
Milch	*milk*
Käse	*cheese*
Orangensaft	*orange juice*
Marmelade	*jam*
Eier	*eggs*
Limonade	*lemonade*
Mineralwasser	*mineral water*
Jogurt	*yoghurt*
Kekse	*biscuits*
Kartoffelsalat	*potato salad*
Schinken	*ham*
Orangen	*oranges*

Im Café	***In the café***
Ich nehme ...	*I'll have ...*
ein Käsebrot	*a cheese sandwich*
einen Hamburger mit Pommes	*a hamburger with chips*
eine Pizza mit Salat	*a pizza with salad*
Apfelstrudel	*apple strudel*
Schwarzwälder Kirschtorte	*Black Forest gateau*
Pflaumenkuchen	*plum cake*
ein Vanilleeis	*a vanilla ice cream*
ein Schokoladeneis	*a chocolate ice cream*
ein Erdbeereis	*a strawberry ice cream*
eine Cola	*a cola*
einen Tee	*a tea*
einen Kaffee	*a coffee*
eine heiße Schokolade mit Sahne	*a hot chocolate with cream*

Kannst du …? Checklist

This is a checklist of the things you should aim to learn in German using Klasse! neu 1.
Use the **Check** boxes and the **Prove it!** column to keep track of what you have learned.

- ★ Tick the first box when you feel you are getting to grips with the learning objective, but sometimes need a prompt or time to think.
- ★ Tick the second box when you think you have fully mastered the learning objective and will be able to use it again in future.
- ★ Make notes following the prompts in the **Prove it!** column to help you show what you have learned. Your learning partner or parent can test you and initial the second box to confirm the progress you have made.

Learning objectives	Check		Prove it!
I can ask what the weather is like.	☐	☐	*Get partner to test you.*
I can describe the weather.	☐	☐	*Get partner to test you.*
I can say what I do depending on the weather.	☐	☐	*Get partner to test you.*
I can use the correct word order after *wenn.*	☐	☐	*Get partner to test you.*
I can make plans for going out.	☐	☐	*Get partner to test you.*
I can ask what somebody wants to do.	☐	☐	*Get partner to test you.*
I can arrange to meet.	☐	☐	*Get partner to test you.*
I can use modal verbs *können* and *wollen.*	☐	☐	*Get partner to test you.*
I can talk about German money.	☐	☐	*Get partner to test you.*
I can ask and say how much something costs.	☐	☐	*Get partner to test you.*
I can say what I want to buy.	☐	☐	*Get partner to test you.*
I can order food and drink in a café.	☐	☐	*Get partner to test you.*
I can use more polite language.	☐	☐	*Get partner to test you.*

Heute Abend fahre ich in die Stadt!

1 **Füll die Lücken aus.**
Fill in the gaps.

Ich fahre …

a zu__ H__l__ __nb__ __

b zu__ Sp__r__z__ __t__um

c z__ __ Sc__ __l__

d z__ __ K__ __o

e z__r D__ __c__

f zu__ P__ __k

2 **Finde die passenden Wörter und schreib Sätze.**
Follow the lines and write sentences.

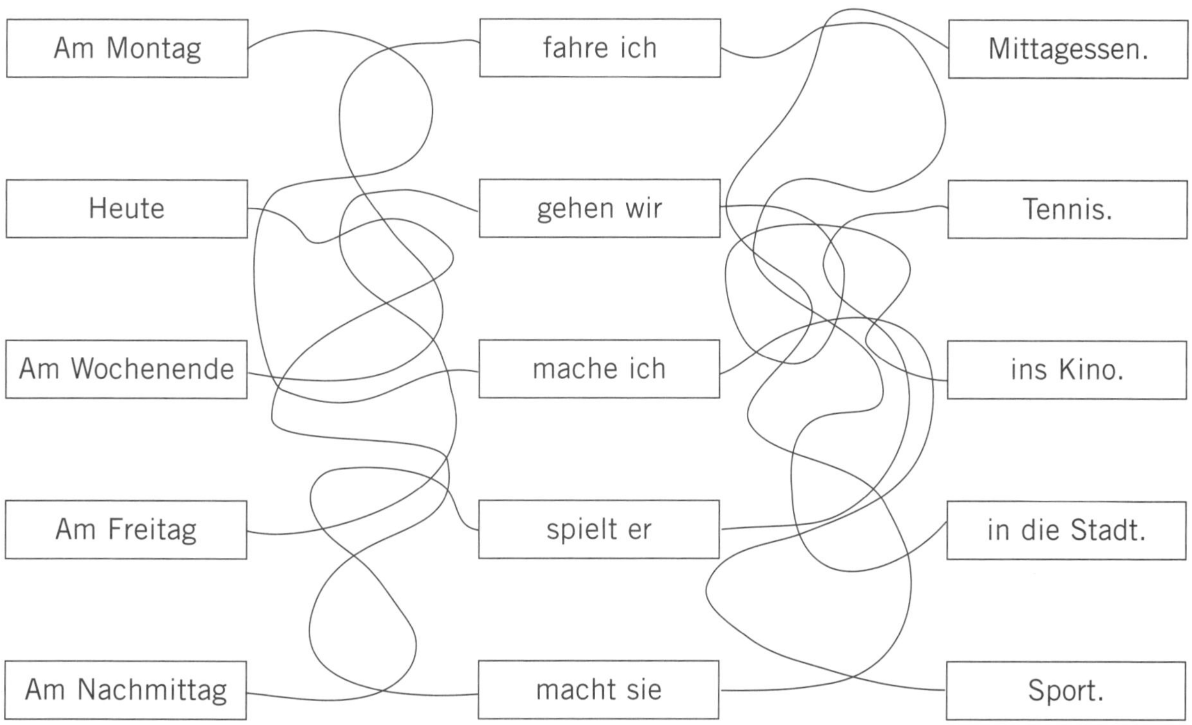

a Am Montag mache ich Sport.

b ______

c ______

d ______

e ______

Was machst du am Wochenende?

1 Finde die passenden Sätze.

Draw lines to match the German sentences with the English ones.

a Ich spiele Tennis.	**1** I do sport.
b Ich habe im Internet gesurft.	**2** I play tennis.
c Ich habe Pizza gemacht.	**3** I cooked.
d Ich höre Musik.	**4** I listen to music.
e Ich mache Sport.	**5** I made pizza.
f Ich habe gekocht.	**6** I surfed the Internet.

2 Kreuz die passenden Wörter an.

Tick the correct words.

1 Ich habe Salat	**a** gemacht.	☐	**4** Ich habe Musik	**a** gesurft.	☐
	b gehört.	☐		**b** gehört.	☐
2 Ich habe im Internet	**a** gekocht.	☐	**5** Ich habe Sport	**a** gemacht.	☐
	b gesurft.	☐		**b** gekocht.	☐
3 Ich habe Mittagessen	**a** gehört.	☐	**6** Ich habe einen Auflauf	**a** gehört.	☐
	b gekocht.	☐		**b** gekocht.	☐

3 Schreib Sätze.

Write sentences.

Beispiel: Am Montag habe ich Fußball gespielt.

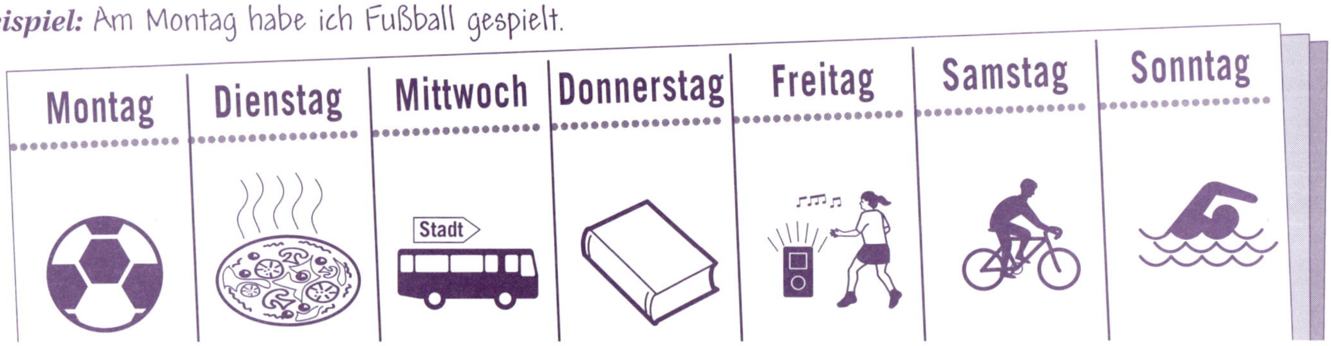

____

____

____

____

____

Was hast du am Samstag gemacht?

1 **Finde die passenden Wörter.**
Draw lines to match the sentence halves.

1	Ich habe Karten	a	gemacht.
2	Ich habe Souvenirs	b	gehört.
3	Ich habe Mittagessen	c	gespielt.
4	Ich habe Pizza	d	getanzt.
5	Ich habe Musik	e	gekauft.
6	Ich habe in der Disco	f	gegessen.

2 **Was haben sie am Wochenende gemacht? Füll die Lücken aus.**
What did they do at the weekend? Fill in the gaps.

gemacht	gespielt
gespielt	gemacht
gekauft	gegessen

a

b

c

d

e

f

Sonntag im Park

1 **Schreib die fünf Sätze richtig auf.**
Find five sentences and write them down.

1 Ich bin ... ________________________________
____ .
2 ____
____ .
3 ____
____ .
4 ____
____ .
5 ____
____ .

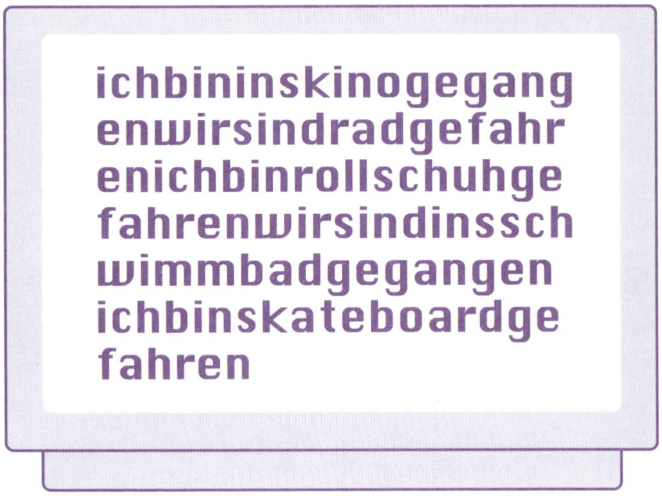

2 **Was hat Tom am Wochenende gemacht? Füll die Sprechblasen aus.**
Fill in the speech bubbles.

getanzt	gehört
gemacht	gegangen
gefahren	

Flashback

			haben		**past participle**
Ich tanze in der Disco.	→	Ich	habe	in der Disco	getanzt.
Du hörst Musik.	→	Du	hast	Musik	gehört.
Wir kaufen CDs.	→	Wir	haben	CDs	gekauft.
			!		
Ich esse ein Eis.	→	Ich	habe	ein Eis	gegessen.

1 **Schreib die Sätze richtig auf.**
Write the sentences correctly.

a haben | Wir | Tennis | gespielt | . ______________________

b eine | gekauft | Ich | Cola | habe | . ______________________

c Nudelsalat | haben | gemacht | Wir | . ______________________

d Wir | der | getanzt | haben | Disco | in | . ______________________

e gehört | Ich | Musik | habe | . ______________________

f frites | Wir | gegessen | haben | Pommes | . ______________________

2 **Füll die Lücken aus.**
Fill in the gaps with the words in the box.

a Ich habe ein Eis ______________________ .

b Wir haben in der Disco ______________________ .

c Ich habe Pizza mit Spinat ______________________ .

d Wir haben eine CD ______________________ .

e Ich habe Basketball ______________________ .

f Wir haben Musik ______________________ .

gespielt	gemacht	gehört	gegessen	getanzt	gekauft

Grammatik 2

Flashback

			sein		past participle
Ich fahre ins Kino.	→	Ich	bin	ins Kino	gefahren.
Du gehst zum Konzert.	→	Du	bist	zum Konzert	gegangen.
Wir gehen zum Park.	→	Wir	sind	zum Park	gegangen.

1 **Finde die passenden Bilder.**
Draw lines to match the pictures to the sentences.

1 

2 

3 

4 

5 

6 

a Ich bin Rollschuh gefahren.

b Wir sind ins Kino gegangen.

c Ich bin zum Sportzentrum gefahren.

d Ich bin zum Park gegangen.

e Wir sind Skateboard gefahren.

f Wir sind zum Konzert gegangen.

2 ***sein*** **oder** ***haben*****? Finde die passenden Wörter.**
Underline the correct verbs.

a Wir haben/sind zur Schule gefahren.

b Ich bin/habe Volleyball gespielt.

c Wir sind/haben einen Spaziergang gemacht.

d Ich habe/bin in die Stadt gegangen.

e Wir haben/sind zum Park gefahren.

f Ich bin/habe ein Erdbeereis gegessen.

Was hast du letzten Samstag/gestern gemacht?	***What did you do last Saturday/yesterday?***
Ich habe ...	*I ...*
(Mittagessen) gekocht.	*cooked (lunch).*
Pizza/Pommes frites mit Würstchen gemacht.	*made pizza/chips with sausages.*
Musik gehört.	*listened to music.*
im Internet gesurft.	*surfed the internet.*
einen Quiz/Sport/Surfboarding gemacht.	*did a quiz/sports/surfboarding.*
Was hast du am Wochenende gemacht?	***What did you do at the weekend?***
Ich habe ...	*I ...*
Wir haben ...	*We ...*
Fußball/Tennis/Karten gespielt.	*played football/tennis/cards.*
Souvenirs/CDs gekauft.	*bought souvenirs/CDs.*
in der Disco getanzt.	*danced in the disco.*
Mittagessen gemacht.	*made lunch.*
Pizza gegessen.	*ate pizza.*
Sonntag im Park	***Sunday in the park***
Ich bin .../Wir sind ...	*I .../We ...*
zum Park/Skateboard gefahren.	*went to the park/did skateboarding.*
ins Kino/zum Konzert gegangen.	*went to the cinema/concert.*
Ich habe .../Wir haben ...	*I .../We ...*
ein Picknick/einen Spaziergang gemacht.	*had a picnic/went for a walk.*
Kakao und Cola getrunken.	*drank hot chocolate and coke.*
eine Band gehört.	*listened to a band.*

Kannst du …? Checklist

This is a checklist of the things you should aim to learn in German using Klasse! neu 1.
Use the **Check** boxes and the **Prove it!** column to keep track of what you have learned.

- ★ Tick the first box when you feel you are getting to grips with the learning objective, but sometimes need a prompt or time to think.
- ★ Tick the second box when you think you have fully mastered the learning objective and will be able to use it again in future.
- ★ Make notes following the prompts in the **Prove it!** column to help you show what you have learned. Your learning partner or parent can test you and initial the second box to confirm the progress you have made.

Learning objectives	**Check**		**Prove it!**
I can describe what I do at the weekend.	☐	☐	*Get partner to test you.*
I can ask what someone did at the weekend.	☐	☐	*Get partner to test you.*
I can say what I did last weekend.	☐	☐	*Get partner to test you.*
I can talk about where I went last weekend.	☐	☐	*Get partner to test you.*
I can compare actions in the present and the past.	☐	☐	*Get partner to test you.*
I can recognize and use the perfect tense with *haben.*	☐	☐	*Get partner to test you.*
I can recognize and use the past tense with *sein.*	☐	☐	*Get partner to test you.*
I can use words to add detail.	☐	☐	*Get partner to test you.*
I can use the correct word order – TIME – MANNER – PLACE.	☐	☐	*Get partner to test you.*

Meine neuen Wörter

Klasse! neu 1 is the first stage of a revised edition of the popular course. Designed to provide a clear, fully-supported and flexible approach to teaching the Modern Languages Framework, this new edition should appeal to all learners.

Klasse! neu 1 *Noch mal!* Workbook complements the Students' Book, providing additional support and language practice. It is ideal for homework and independent classroom study.

This workbook provides:

- extra practice material for the key language and Framework objectives launched in each unit
- pages to consolidate key grammar points
- a vocabulary list for each unit
- unit checklists, for pupils to record their own progress.

Students' Book 1	0 19 840644 4
Noch mal! 1 Workbook	**0 19 840646 0**
Extra! 1 Workbook	0 19 840647 9
Teacher's Book 1	0 19 840645 2
Copymaster Book 1	0 19 840650 9
Set of CDs 1	0 19 840642 8
Set of cassettes 1	0 19 840648 7
OHT File 1	0 19 840643 6
Flashcards (Parts 1–2)	0 19 912498 1*
Coursemaster CD-ROM	0 19 840651 7
Klasse! neu 1 Integral Teacher's edition	0 19 912595 3
Klasse! neu 1 Integral Students' edition	0 19 912594 5

**as per original set*

OXFORD
UNIVERSITY PRESS

www.OxfordSecondary.co.uk

Orders and enquiries to Customer Services:
tel. 01536 741068 fax 01536 454519

ISBN 0-19-840646-0

9 780198 406464